SIGNS OF AGNI YOGA
INFINITY
II

INFINITY

II

1930

Agni Yoga Society
319 West 107th Street
New York NY 10025
www.agniyoga.org

© 1957 by the Agni Yoga Society.
Published 1957.
Reprinted 2017.
Translated from Russian by the Agni Yoga Society.

ISBN: 978-1-946742-81-0
ISBN (eBook): 978-1-946742-09-4

INFINITY
Part II

1. The core of the planet is surrounded with energies which infuse life into all its processes. But in tensity the planet has varied from its original saturation. Indeed, it cannot be denied that the two poles are out of balance. The counter-position is a result of their having one and the same source. Each encirclement of the planet brings an accumulation of energy.

In the planetary dimension and in the spiritual the forces of attraction are identical; hence, a specific combination issues from each contact and creative striving results. The creation of conditions depends upon the attraction of the impelled seeds. The spirit creates seeds through its striving. Thus the ocean of Infinity is within each seed.

2. The currents are transforming the Earth and generating a new step. The manifestation of a date evokes all alternate currents. All dormant energies are aroused; all subject to destruction is strained. Shall the heart not quiver when the flame of conflagration engulfs all spheres? All the departing and all self-asserting energies are determining their tension. The East awakens and opposes the West; the North opposes the South—and shall the heart not quiver? Ominous are the currents, and the spirit assimilates all courses. The cosmic verdict is austere but full of limitless beauty. As We in the Tower follow the gathering of new threads, you also must perceive all movements of the element of Fire.

Verily, the centers of an Agni Yogi feel each planetary vibration. Hence, it is so imperative to strive toward Us during the cosmic perturbations. Just as We share in the destiny of the planet, so We also partake of the beauty of the Infinite.

3. The aura of man, affirmed for cosmic transmissions, depends upon various conditions just as does a conductor of electricity. When the human spheres require certain shocks, the cosmic transmissions flow accordingly. Only those elements adhere to the spheres which can be absorbed by the affirmed auras. When spheres require violent destruction, those spheres cannot absorb the streaming transmissions of Cosmos. Hence, the darkness surrounding the planet will never permit the affirmation without the manifestation of explosions. These forces of purification will illumine humanity. The cosmic fires attract the affirmed dates.

4. The purifying fires of the Universe penetrate all regions of the planet. The sparks of conflagration spread along all channels of karmic action. As volcanoes, these affirmed fires explode. The force of karma shifts and transfers power from hand to hand. The cosmic course is directed toward those purifying conflagrations; hence the comet, speeding through the Infinite. The tensity of the currents is very great and the effect corresponds to the fires of the planet. The centers of the Agni Yogi record all cosmic currents.

5. The magnetic currents of the human aura penetrate the most dense regions. Certainly, science must call these emanations psychic energy. Indeed, adjustments should be made in regard to these manifestations of inexhaustible energy. Tensive properties propel the psychic seeds and form a sphere conducive to striving. The nature of the emanations can produce a powerful tension. Depending upon the way the streams of these emanations of a blended aura are directed, the power of this energy is either destructive or constructive. Thus, from human emanations it will be possible to derive the most heterogeneous energies. Conscious handling of the emanations of the human aura will afford an achievement of great fiery creativeness.

6. The irradiation of the human aura can intensify a powerful energy. The propelled stream of a center can melt an intensified energy. Hence, when streams of blue fire pour from the fingers, it is the creativeness of the emanations that manifests the action; thus do the centers create. The spiritual transmissions are intensified by the same energies. All creative processes are thus strained by the centers. The process of creativeness of the centers is so subtle that it is invisible. Of course the centers act creatively on many planes. The creativeness of the propelled irradiation strives into the spheres of the far-off worlds. Creative emanations truly magnetize space.

7. Cosmic creativeness utilizes all vital impulses, straining the most vital levers. Of all impulses, the most powerful is unification. In it is comprised the entire manifestation of life; by it is created the vital combination. Then why not apply this principle to life! When unification battles with differentiation, a powerful explosion occurs. The fragments from this explosion are often projected far apart and these parts then forfeit their power of mutual attraction. Hence, in repelling the forces to which he is connected by karma man generates explosive forces. The law constructs only through unification. The element of attraction indicates the direction for all striving energies. The Brothers of Humanity designate the path for everything which is affirmed by evolution. Thus, the power of attraction is manifested as the law of Be-ness.

8. This cosmic force of unification affirms the power of the Cosmic Reason. You have correctly alluded to the transmissions of the spirit. The creativeness of the spirit intensifies so many inceptions. Therefore, when We speak of spirit creativeness We call this force a ray of Cosmos. Thus, each wave of spirit intensifies vibrations in space.

9. It is customary to ascribe to cosmic creativeness a certain amount of chaos. Humanity formulates its concepts without taking into consideration the quality of cosmic action. When each form demands such tension of creation, why not entertain the thought of an extracting of all the best cosmic impulses by the Magnet? Indeed, Cosmos is constructed from the fiery subtlest of energies. Equal vigilance is applied by Us, Brothers of Humanity, in the laying of better foundations. They will ask, "How, then, do you permit the presence of dark forces in a site destined for purification?" We will say, "Cosmos does not punish; Cosmos does not eject; but in conformance to the law these engenderments do away with themselves." Thus, the portions of the planet which are predestined for regeneration outlive their progeny. The Cosmic Magnet permits each part to be saturated by the currents up to the point of explosion. There are no half measures in Cosmos. Hence, keen eyes can distinguish the departing and the nascent energies. A new form can be molded only in tension. Hence, We will say to him who is perplexed: "strive, sharpening your creative vision, and you will discern easily how the Creative Magnet constructs."

10. When a country is disintegrating, this manifestation may reveal itself in a last efflorescence. These engenderments will contribute to the speeding destruction. Thus acts the Cosmic Magnet, and the currents confirm the advancing affirmation. Our Carriers of Light sense this tension.

11. The substance of the Fire of Space directs the human consciousness. Since it is acknowledged that even the rays of the moon help the growth of plants and affect inanimate objects, one may go a step further and admit the creativeness of the rays. Certainly the sun—the life giver—saturates the entire Universe; but the realization that the streaming rays impart a conscious force of energy will afford the most fiery attainments. Cosmos demands uniformity of striving in all things. Sensing the vibrations of the currents, humanity will discover the multifold creative transmissions of the rays. Thus does Cosmos bestow its treasures. The substantiation of these treasures is inevitable. Spiritual application should be accepted equally with the wondrous powerful impulse. Cosmic creation is built upon the foundation of spirit. A discovery comes in a harmonious fusion with a cosmic ray. The rays from heterogeneous elements bring immeasurable revelations to humanity.

12. If the physicians would become aware of the vibrations of Cosmos, they could discover much that would be useful for healing. A ray may be discovered which would awaken accumulations in the Chalice and thus dispel sluggishness.

13. The law of generation creates its own affirmations. When the properties of the fire coordinate with the attraction of the Cosmic Magnet, space is enriched with a new formula. A man seeking to harmonize his qualities cooperates with Cosmos. In creating his spiritual image, each one adds to the harmonization in Cosmos. The currents of space are reinforced through the principle of fusion. This law rules all cosmic forces. The man who confirms his life path shows cosmic

cooperation. The power of space is calling in self-sacrifice, and self-sacrifice is inscribed in the construction of Cosmos. It is precisely self-sacrifice that guides the light of the spirit into Infinity.

14. The aspects of self-sacrifice are so varied in human understanding that only the highest measurement must be used in everything. He who in self-sacrifice dedicates himself to Service is confirmed as the co-worker of Light. He who serves Cosmic Fire sacrifices himself. He who serves evolution is affirmed as a bearer of the law. He who serves, he who is devoted to the General Good, is confirmed as a co-worker of Cosmos.

The creativeness of the centers reacts to all manifestations of the higher aspects of self-sacrifice. When the transmutation of Fire will enter life, it will be possible to say, "Verily, the Cosmic Ordinance is realized!" Cosmos imbues all lives with Fire, and for a new manifestation one should develop in oneself identical energies. In this identity are comprised all worlds. In this identity is comprised the mission of an Agni Yogi. Hence, the vibrations which the centers of an Agni Yogi assimilate are identical with the fires of space. Thus, I see the invisible creativeness of the centers. By the records of the creative fires one may determine the spirit creativeness.

15. Thus, we shall term the cosmic energy the Breath of Be-ness. The force impelling life is comprised in each atom as inherent to each element, in which the predestined impulse in turn creates a direction. The impelling force magnetizes by its attraction that sphere which surrounds it. As a continuity of action, there will be a generation of other seeds in the sphere. These spheres fill the space, and humanity has its own affirmed combination of spheres. The spirit itself determines its sphere and upon entering it, acts as a magnetic force. The cosmic spheres and the human spheres are subject to the law of Cosmic Breath.

16. The Breath of Cosmos compels human creativity to advance in the direction of evolution. A rhythmic succession is provided by this law. Creativity is directed in a designated rhythm, but the rejecting principle cannot construct a bridge to the rays that are sent. The fiery spirit is aware of the ray's vibration. The fiery spirit assimilates cosmic thought and the Breath of Cosmos. Fiery Spirits stand guard!

17. The sensation of quivering is of course called into being by the currents of subterranean and superterranean fires. The entire condition of tension is attributable to cosmic and planetary currents. Each manifestation of the elements establishes its accord. I ask that all sensations be recorded; these are important indicators. Following explosions there is heaviness. The subterranean fire surges toward the cooled places; hence the manifestation of explosions. If one would observe the direction of motion of the fire of the centers, the direction of the cosmic fires could be discerned.

18. The effect of the surging Fire will provide a new formula for the investigation of the interplanetary spheres. Much is said about a void, this concept being applied to cover all things incomprehensible. Space contains vast expanses of uninvestigated spheres. The rarefaction and densification of the elements is determined not by void but by the power of attraction. There is no place for void where life is being affirmed. All cosmic manifestations vibrate with the power of attraction. The man who believes that invisible thought departs into void is in grievous error. Everything which is in possession of its own potentiality offers limitless results.

19. Invisible thoughts permeate the space and are attracted to different spheres, impregnating them with energies. In the power of impregnation by thought is contained the "Divine Fire" of the ancients. The key of the affirmed impregnation by energy was given as the manifestation of the Cosmic Sacrament. Verily, thought impregnates all Be-ness. Spirit creativeness corresponds to impregnation. It is said that the manifestation of Be-ness has no beginning but that the powerful diffused flame which encompasses Cosmos lives through consciousness.

20. The consciousness which envelopes the seed of the spirit imbues it with the affirmation of the power of Cosmic Fire. The precise striving of the seed of the spirit determines the construction of the manifest fire. The element manifested in the potential of the seed of the spirit transmits the direction to the consciousness. The surrounding of the spirit with strata of striving fires gives it the power to penetrate different spheres. These fine strata afford to the potential of the spirit the possibility of manifesting its striving. The denser layers hold back the potentiality to a great extent. The properties of the accumulated layers indicate a slow or rapid advance toward evolution. The creativeness of the spirit is measured by its potential and by the strata of Fire. The fiery transmutation is saturated with the emanations of space; and the potential of the spirit, which is contained in each cosmic seed, attracts all energies. Each cosmic breath is limitlessly strained by the consciousness.

21. The potential of spirit of Our Brothers comprises in itself energies identical with those of Cosmos. When We strive toward evolution it may be said that the currents of Cosmos bring identical currents. The Fire of Space lives by the same impulse. Indeed We always imply Sisters as well, when speaking of Brothers. The Origins are affirmed as the equilibrium in Cosmos. He who denies the principle of balance affirms imbalance. Cosmic creativeness necessitates the spirit impregnation of one Origin by the other. Thus, the Origins are created in Cosmos for reciprocal creation. The manifestation of reciprocal creation is affirmed as the symbol of Be-ness.

22. The sensing of the quivering of the ground and the sensing of the moving of clouds should be recorded. Subtlety of receptivity is bestowed upon the refined Carrier of the Chalice. The assimilation of subtle fires can yield manifestations attainable in higher spheres.

23. The planetary tension permits the penetration of only those currents which are identical with the atmosphere surrounding the Earth. The currents existing around the Earth obstruct the transmissions of space; thus the spheres engulf the most substantial power. The attraction of these spheres is based upon their substance. These spatial spots are being born as storms and clouds. The emanations of the spheres are the result of human engenderments; the currents of this issue generate their own forms, and humanity wonders how the earthly chastisement occurs. The law of the spheres is immutable, and creativeness is manifested through the highest impulse. Thus, the attraction of the higher sphere is unattainable to the lower sphere. The energies which can contact the spirit possessing the subtle energies will bestow the power of Fire upon humanity. The one who possesses the synthesis will give to the planet the realization of subtle

energies. The cosmic rays, which bring the affirmation of Fire to humanity, are directed toward action.

Thus, Space creates boundlessly!

24. Indeed, the vessel that assimilates the finest energies differs greatly from the usual manifestations, but people are compelled to apply that measure which has the force of their own judgment. The subtle receptivity of hearing is the affirmation of the link of that center with the Fire of Space. The subtle receptivity of the eye is the link of that center with the Fire of Space. The subtle receptivity of all the centers is the link with the Fire of Space. Each manifestation of the Fire of Space can respond to all vibrations of the centers. Cosmic creativeness comprises in itself help to humanity. Each concordance confirms a new step for humanity. Therefore, the centers of an Agni Yogi, encompassing the help for humanity, are strained. When an Agni Yogi feels the quivering of the Earth, it means that the process of the movement of the Fire may be traced.

During the shifting of the subterranean fire the superterranean currents are heavy and the sensitive organism feels strain, anguish and the affirmation of a fiery manifestation. Therefore, the shiftings of Fire are so difficult. Thus should we remember!

25. It may be said that Cosmos is in a perpetual state of fiery transmutation. The law and the motion are established by reciprocal attraction. Each energy attracted to the striving seed produces its effect. These effects enwrap the entire planet. Certainly the discovered law of electricity is connected with the Fire of Space. Indeed, all manifestations of cosmic records abroad in space are open to human understanding. Knowledge is so relative that humanity must embrace the cosmic understanding with a universal eye. The creativeness of a fiery transmutation is based upon the striving of the fire toward the higher intensity. These cosmic seeds are strongly attracted toward the magnet of the form. Space abounds in these seeds.

26. The spark which kindles creativeness is inherent in the very seed of the spirit. The basis of cosmic creativeness is established upon this principle. The limitation of human thought directs man into the spheres separated from the designated path. In antiquity the communion with the Fire of Space was known and the departure which affirmed a new life was venerated. The entire essence of Be-ness is contained in this law of communion with the Fire of Space and in the principle of interchange of energies. Observing sensitively the manifestation of energies, one may note what the impulses are which activate the energies. As in a chemical reaction the properties of the energies are distinctive, so also the properties of the impulses of spirit must be observed. The impulses of children can afford the best indications. One can direct the impulse to a reaction and can induce it to take on a new tone. One may observe how a child, having lost one such impulse, will apply a new energy to his spirit. In the great laboratory of Cosmos all the heterogeneous elements may be applied. But humanity has lost its possibilities to such an extent that it is impossible to affirm such interrelation without explosion.

27. Cosmos is maintained upon interrelations. The force of attraction is an acting power as well as the power of cohesion. Upon the basis of the manifestation of attraction alone does the great law verily prevail. As material bodies act through the forces of attraction, so the entire spiritual world exists by the same law. Through this alone is life suffused by the creative impulse. The cosmic equation is based upon the equation of the chain of continuity.

You have spoken correctly about Hierarchy. Indeed, the spiral of life is built only upon this principle. The creativity of the Teacher likewise is manifested in eternal motion; therefore, the imbuing of the disciple must proceed with the creativity of the Teacher. Hence, the disciple who enumerates his attainments casts himself beyond the bounds of truth. Therefore, I will say that there is only one Shield—Hierarchy. Therefore, the disciple who considers his soft arm-chair higher than the throne of the Guru must verily remember the Giving Hand. I deplore it when a self-asserting disciple acts in arrogance.

We consider haughtiness toward one's Guru as the limit of conceit. Thus let the disciples remember on all paths.

28. The Fire of Space kindles the manifestations of propulsive energies. The manifestation of spatial torches is to be found throughout Cosmos. The human consciousness is kindled by the torches of the Fire of Space. Each spirit bearing fire in its potential is such a torch. The most fiery torch directs humanity to the assimilation of the affirmation of the spiritual fire. The creativeness of these torches intensifies the thought in a spatial scope. The Fire of Space, which imbues the Universe, creates the manifestations of energies as evolution. The torch of spiritual consciousness offers its intensified spiral to humanity. Along this spiral moves the affirmed life. The torch which creates the spiral of thought verily calls to the Fire of Space. Thus, We shall say to the striving ones: "Be like torches!"

29. How ominous is the new time, how beautiful is the new time! The purification of space is intensified by the fiery torch. The striving torches of the Agni Yogi imbue the space, and the action of the affirmed shifting of the Cosmic Magnet begins to be felt. In the process of assembling a new race, and at the foundation of the New Era, the manifestations of the affirmed purifications take place along with the explosions. Only the cognition of the Fire of Space will give humanity the understanding of the essence. Thus is the cosmic life built. Therefore, when the spirit of the people is saturated with Fire, purification is inevitable. The Agni Yogi creates like a fiery torch and propels the consciousness forward. Without these fires it is impossible to shift the consciousness. I so attest. Yes, yes, yes!

The time approaches for the final reckoning. The shifting proceeds; therefore the planet is atremble. Hence, the sensitive organism of the Agni Yogi feels it. The sensitive organism of the Agni Yogi knows that wondrous step. Since the ominous time is governed by the Magnet, it may be said that pure Fire is transmuting the forms. I so attest!

30. Upon the evolutionary path energies strive toward the process of perfection. The manifestations of forms, being subject to the impulse of evolution, fuse in space. In this impulse there is a conscious process. The creativity of the Cosmic Magnet proceeds by way of conscious perfecting. Only by way of the higher process may one approach the creativeness of Cosmos. How, then, is it possible not to accept progress by way of perfecting? When the spirit is aware of an infinite path, each movement should breathe with striving.

31. The one-sided understanding of man carries him into a closed circle from which there is no outlet. Having failed to accept the affirmation of Truth, man has thereby deprived himself of the path of self-perfecting. Hence, when the manifestation of destruction approaches, there is no way out of the closed circle. Therefore, the evolving spirit inevitably attains the striving for the manifestation of Fire. Therefore, those who are imbued with the Truth of Our Teaching establish the affirmation of fiery evolution. Thus, the Carriers of Fire imbue evolution with creativeness. Therefore, the assertion of the fire of the centers is Our manifestation. Therefore, when We say that all which is affirmed by Us is the highest ordainment, it means that the Cosmic Magnet is thus expressing its Will. Thus let us remember.

It is difficult but wondrous!

32. In Cosmos the center of striving rests upon the principle of Hierarchy. Cosmos acts by means of attraction to the manifested powerful center. Thus the cosmic seed is manifested in each action of Hierarchy by the quality of the striving, which ascends through realization of the predominant principle. Cosmic creativeness brings together the harmonious energies. This principle is so important that it is an undeniable necessity, which is truly affirmed by the principle of Hierarchy. The entire Universe is saturated with this principle. This spirit, which imbues all cosmic manifestations on the planet, is affirmed by the Highest Reason. Therefore, man, being a part of Cosmos, cannot separate himself from this principle. When cosmic creativeness is imbued with Reason, each manifestation of the Infinite is affirmed by the same principle.

33. The strivings of Cosmos are manifested upon this principle. When Our Brothers of Humanity adhere to the cosmic creativeness, the principle of unity is affirmed. The property of intense fire contains in itself the property of unification. The inherent impulse of striving attracts the atom toward consummation. The union with the Highest Reason is followed by cosmic fusion. The Crown of Be-ness unites that which belongs to it. The Highest Reason blends that which it manifests. The Cosmic Magnet fuses that which it gathers. Thus triumphs the beauty of Be-ness!

34. Cosmic blending is tensed by the Fire of Space. The fusion of sparks is precipitated by the Cosmic Magnet. Fiery seeds live in each atom, and the power of cohesion rests in these fiery seeds. When the intensified force of the creative Magnet is acting, the fire of the seed fuses with the impulsion of the Magnet. The manifested fire breathes the impulse of life into each atom. The spirit creativeness is strained by the manifestation of Fire. When thoughts create spiritually at a distance, such action is analogous to the creativity of the Fire of Space. The reception and the transmission are under the same law. The action of Fire is comprised in the impulsion of the Magnet. Hence, the magnet of the spirit reflects all cosmic manifestations. These potential forces are established by the Reason as the life force. The magnet of the spirit combines all vital impulses. Indeed, the magnet of the spirit fuses matter even physically. Of course, the treasury of the spirit is the Chalice, and that treasury also guards matter, because the powerful impulse of sacred Fire is laid in it. Thus, a wise power flows from the seed of the Fire of Space. Thus, the seed of the spirit intensifies the striving toward the higher spheres.

35. The magnet of the spirit, this propellent aggregator of the life energies, is nurtured by the manifestation of the cosmic energy. The accumulations in the Chalice gather around the seed of the spirit, enveloping it in their colors. The very striving seed of the spirit responds to the fiery impulsion. Thus, the magnet of the spirit of an Agni Yogi is the creative sower of the affirmed fires. Verily, the sower of cosmic fires into the consciousness of men is a true co-worker of Cosmos.

Humanity will acknowledge the Carriers of Fire!

36. Reality responds to intensity. When the striving of the energies aggregates around the seed, reality creates. In regard to illusion, this law has been forgotten. In reality Light engulfs darkness. The fusion of energies is consummated in reality. When cosmic creativeness intensifies reality, the entire power of attraction is applied. Reality is imbued with magnetic currents. The presence of striving affords a powerful flux of attraction. Only these processes give rise to the manifestation of life. Constant striving into a higher sphere produces the tension of reality. The inalienable attraction of the Cosmic Magnet sustains humanity on its path of evolution. The countless courses of reality are confirmed by the law of Infinity.

37. Only a minor part of reality is cognized by humanity. The Cosmic Eye is tensed in contemplation of reality. Humanity dwells in a restricted reality; in the human conception reality is limited to that which is visible. Space testifies to the correlation of processes and effects. Hence, while a process may be confined to the invisible spheres, it nevertheless creates reality. The law of fiery transmutation pertains to the same creativeness of Fire. Hence, the centers create invisibly. This psycho-creative reality intensifies all vital actions. Therefore, the transmissions of spirit and thought through the fiery centers imbue the space.

38. Evolution, directed toward the erection of a new step, is affirmed in the annunciation of Fire. The planet is discarding all outworn energies. The surrounding encumbrances in space may be removed only by the subtle energies. The power that gave life to the energies receives for reaffirmation these energies which it must transmute. Thus are the cosmic energies generated and shifted. So is it also with the human spirit. Humanity eliminates its outworn energies. Hence, when the

action of the battle reaches its peak, space carries away the old remnants and asserts the New Truth. Thus are the cosmic cycles established. The fulfillment of the designated dates lies in that replacement, and the rhythm of the cycles is created by the assertion of these alterations. The law of Infinity replaces one by another.

39. All that is outworn is subject to the law of replacement. All that does not progress is subject to the law of replacement. The cosmic creativeness so definitely foresees the utilization of the energies that it substitutes one for the other, without delay. In each vital manifestation one must observe the identical replacements. When the spirit is not dominated by its accumulations, it creates under the strain of its karma and of the creative impulse. All accumulations which are not outlived will consign the spirit to the Fire for a process of long duration. The spirit which has readily replaced its cumulations will be a vessel for the Fire. The spirit will express the intensity of the striving. The refined assimilation of transmutation will accord the knowledge of replacement. The ray of the Agni Yogi gives direction to striving.

40. The cosmic pulse governs all manifestations of life. The failure to adhere to the rhythm of this pulsation acts as a diversion of striving. The cosmic pulsation governs the generating of energies as well as their shifting. The cosmic pulsation governs the destinies of nations and precipitates the fate of the planet. Cosmic pulsation designates the path of evolution and the dates of the shiftings. A magnetized spiral asserts itself in streams of Cosmic Fire. The manifestation of imbalance results from the action of the Fire of Space. When the spiral in its motion meets a counteraction, the cosmic pulsation is violated. How greatly does humanity interrupt the cosmic pulsation by its course, which is seemingly toward evolution but is not true progress! The cosmic pulsation creates as a straining spiral. Humanity creates as a flattened spiral. Can one then expect progress toward evolution when there is such a great disparity between these manifestations! Only the thought which is saturated with the emanations of pure Fire produces an intense spiral. Thought is the seed of spirit and of action. The labor which expands with the pulsation of Cosmos is affirmed as progress into evolution.

41. The cosmic pulsation that is sensed by the heart is the most wondrous vibration. All complex problems of Cosmos can be solved by the heart. When the rhythm of Mahavan is sensed by the heart of an Agni Yogi, the union with the cosmic pulsation follows. The Spatial Fire, impelled to action, transmits currents to the heart. The Mother of Agni Yoga, having given herself to the Cosmic Service, verily cooperates cosmically.

42. The fusion of energies are manifested in different spheres. When a lower sphere is taut for fusion, an identical energy approaches it. The higher sphere summons the higher energy. Similarly are the human fields of action divided. Those who cling to the lower sphere preordain their own destinies. Each assimilation and each response thus affirms the tension of the spirit. These indicators subtly define the striving of the spirit.

43. When the centers are strained and the fire manifests itself as a sun, special precautions must be taken. The indicator of the creativeness of the centers is in their tension. The subtle assimilation evokes tension. The fires of the centers which were seen by the Agni Yogi testify to the amount of Fire present. Hence, the energy of the centers must be protected.

44. Cosmic creativeness constructs all world steps by the attraction of the Magnet, and spirit is implanted in the potentiality of all creation. When cosmic forces are strained in creativeness, it is spirit that is acting. When creativeness aggregates its parts, it is spirit that is acting. When a cosmic sphere is regenerated, spirit is acting. The Spatial Fire that is attracted to a destined element is directed by spirit. Why, then, not apply to human activity the creativeness of spirit? One should regard consciously the constructive impulse.

45. The essence of the attraction of the Cosmic Magnet is contained in the assertion of new combinations. The power of the Cosmic Magnet exerts strain upon those parts of the energies which are not united. Upon this process of fusion the entire cosmic creativity is built. Wherever the eye turns, life is being built by these processes. Spheres are formed around the seed of spirit and around the cosmic seed; and the cosmic seed constructs the spheres,. Thus do the cosmic energies mutually create. Upon this creativity stands the Infinity.

46. Of course, every cosmic manifestation sets up a tensed spiral in the Agni Yogi; that is why there is such a tension of the centers. Great caution must be applied in regard to the centers.

47. The yearning for manifestation is expressed by all straining energies. Thus, upon all planes the striving arising from this stimulus may be observed. This is the stimulus that evokes manifestations; it is the assembling stimulus; it is the life-asserting stimulus. All manifestations of this stimulus are intensified by the magnet of life. Each conscious striving is steered by this lever. The Spatial Fire which imbues each seed asserts this stimulus. That is why the construction of Cosmos is so precipitant. Only the magnet attraction can create new forms. The cosmic creativeness is greatly intensified by this powerful stimulus. Thus are the parts of identical energies assembled.

48. A great Oneness reigns in Cosmos as a powerful law. Only those who adhere to this law can verily take part in cosmic cooperation. The Oneness of substance in everything urges humanity to creativity. When the consciousness draws from the treasury of Space, the Cosmic Magnet is under tension. The manifested treasury contains the expression of the energy imbued by the Oneness. Therefore each seed of the spirit must feel this Oneness. Each seed of the spirit belongs to the Cosmic Oneness in which all cosmic creativeness is comprised. Humanity deprives itself in departing from this truth by setting up a law of separateness. Immutable is the law of the Oneness in infinite diversity!

Only by this law can one build, because when attraction is creating, the power that lies in the action is Oneness. The creativity of Cosmos is boundless through this Oneness!

49. Upon Oneness stands the entire affirmed Be-ness. The operating law is so stupendous that all cosmic construction rests upon this principle. In every manifestation this law assembles the parts, uniting those which belong to each other. This great law is the Crown of Cosmos.

50. In the eternal creativeness of life, the law of Oneness holds. The cosmic creativeness goes forth as a fiery command; a command preordaining fusion; a command preordaining destiny; a command preordaining the replacement of one by another; a command preordaining consummation; a command preordaining immortality; a command preordaining life for each atom; a command preordaining the approach of new energy; a command preordaining the New Era. Thus is the cosmic creation accomplished by the magnet of life. How then is it possible to split the creation of the Cosmos? How then can those things which belong to one another be separated? How then can those things which verily issue one from another be separated? Indeed, in its saturation Cosmos is strained for the fiery fusion! Only Cosmic Reason can give to humanity the Image of Oneness. Reason gives to humanity the supreme Image of the creation of the most fiery Heart. Reason assembles in sacredness; therefore, in Cosmos this law is created by life. Where then is the end, when all cosmic manifestations evolve upon two Origins? When a spirit contacts the higher spheres, cosmic creativeness is revealed to it as the law of infinite unity. When the spirit reaches the highest Oneness, it may be said verily that it draws from the vessel of cosmic joy. Yes, yes, yes!

51. The spirit shudders at the thought of death. But when consciousness penetrates the essence of Be-ness, the conception of Oneness is confirmed. When the spirit understands how ceaselessly the manifestations of life flow, the continuity of all chains may be indicated. The chain of thought, the chain of action, the chain of effects, the chain of strivings, the chain of lives—each chain predetermines the succeeding one. The creativeness of the magnet of life lies in these chains. The spirit must shudder not at the thought of death and change but at the thought of sundering the chain. If one could observe the records of disrupted chains borne in space, the spirit verily would shudder. When the great shifting is brought about, only he will succeed who has adhered to the oneness of evolution.

52. How much striving is dissipated by humanity in the search for phenomena, without heed to the

voice which directs it toward the power of spirit-understanding. Does the materialization of objects have such powerful attraction that the understanding of the transmissions of spirit and energy can be erased? How can materialization, which suffocates the consciousness and which leads only to visible manifestations, direct the spirit to the far-off worlds? Each manifested form is of itself a cosmic phenomenon. Humanity has arrested itself upon the step of search for visible manifestations. In speaking of the far-off worlds, one should accept the entire broad understanding of infinite growth. Let us confirm our consciousness upon the thought of the far-off worlds. The stimulus of spirit creativeness comprises the entire boundlessness of striving. In it is preserved the great cosmic striving. Only with the understanding of invisible materialization can there be true striving, because in that great impulse of the Universe is comprised the entire cosmic creativeness.

53. Since everything is transmuted in cosmic creativity, humanity can apply the cosmic laws very easily. Acceptance of the law of evolution will readily reveal the understanding of the law of cosmic progress of the spirit. It will then be possible to approach the path leading to the far-off worlds. Can humanity, which lives only in the world of effects, make progress? Losing sight of the world of causes, humanity has certainly lost the bond with the law of Existence. Only the chain of lives can give the understanding of the cause of lives. Therefore, when We say that the spirit which is consummating its path has prepared its body through millennia, this is a true assertion. All causes of the spirit's strivings create their effects, and in this law of Oneness is comprised the entire cosmic creativeness.

54. If humanity would comprehend the purpose of

being, it could then join in the cosmic creativity. How can one advance without realization of the eternal cosmic shifting? Only when strivings are manifested beyond the limits revealed by life can one perceive cosmic creativeness. A wall of folly has formed; the mist of contentment is like a screen. When it will be possible to penetrate the spheres of true cosmic creativeness, the Cosmic Consciousness will be manifested. Alongside the creativity of Cosmos, the human spirit, which is a part of it, is active. Cosmic balance demands striving toward limitless perfecting. Hence, when the spirit of humanity cooperates with the Cosmic Magnet, it is itself drawn to that boundary which will assist it in striving into the Infinite. Thus, beyond the wall of its contentment, humanity prepares for itself the boundary of Cosmic Justice.

55. You are correct in speaking of humanity's lack of insight. When we approach the ominous hour, all forces must be strained for the mighty step. It has already been told that the Epoch of Maitreya is approaching, and the signs are strewn as fiery seeds; hence, the ominous hour will be one of Light for those who are in step with the Cosmic Magnet. Hence, the ominous hour will be as a future Light for those who battle for the significance of the Epoch of Maitreya. Hence, cooperation with Us brings the predestined victory. Therefore, the co-workers who walk in self-denial will be victors. Proceeding in step with the Cosmic Magnet, you affirm victory! Yes, yes, yes!

56. Humanity regards all uninvestigated energies as nonexistent. It is not striving but denial that impels humanity to reject the subtlest energies. When the cosmic creativeness strains its levers, the pre-ordained forms are generated. But humanity, in not aspiring to accept the new forms, certainly rejects further progress. Everything soars around humanity, but the energies only then take form when they come in contact with the human consciousness. Hence the surging tide toward deaf receivers is bringing but isolation from the cosmic treasury. Thus humanity deprives itself of the most precious.

57. Verily, the new energies are directed toward the perfection of life. When humanity will accept the concept of Spatial Fire, it will understand how the generation of new energies proceeds. When We speak of the Spatial Fire, We have in mind those seeds which affirm life and which strain all forms toward manifestation. That is why the receptivity of the Agni Yogi is so fiery. That is why the striving toward the cosmic current is so manifest. Hence, I affirm that the higher receptivity of the centers is manifested for the assimilation of the highest. Thus, I affirm that the centers will bestow upon humanity a new valuable science.

58. True attainments are attested by the striving to cognize the Will of Highest Reason. It is difficult to accept a cosmic direction without understanding the Will of Highest Reason. Three-fourths of human strivings are directed against Cosmic Ordainments. The human spirit is not penetrating beyond the boundaries of visibility, and the opposition to the Will of Reason is leading to destruction. True, cosmic law ordains the replacement of one thing by another. Certainly, in this ordinance is contained the spirit of renewal. Certainly, the principle of renewal comprises in itself the law of perfection. Therefore, the shifting asserted by humanity advances very slowly into evolution. The potentiality of the past gives birth to the future. Immeasurable is the growth of potentiality! There where the shifting leads to new progress, all forces are strained. There where the past was imbued with opposition, cosmic

purification is established. Thus, the shifting of the manifested epoch of destruction will assert its consequences. They are inevitable, and the potentiality will erect its step.

59. In the flowering of the potential of spirit we see the synthesis. How powerfully this blossoming of the potential proceeds, and how continuously it is directed toward the consummation! The manifestation of the consummation magnetizes the entire chain of lives for that spirit who knows cosmic law. The affirmation of Be-ness thus leads the spirit. At the cosmic fusion the law must lead, and, having contacted the vibration of the Cosmic Magnet, the striving spirit cleaves in its essence to the ordinance of fusion.

60. One should seek Truth beyond the boundaries of human understanding. The destruction of the broad fields of vision, the cosmic, has not led to progress. When thought dwelt in the lower sphere, the striving manifested was in conformity with the scope of this sphere. When instead of a striving for expansion there was substituted the striving toward a limited sphere, that of the visible, the horizon indeed was narrowed. Cosmic creativeness aggregates its manifested forms according to expressed affinity. The attraction of correlated particles by the Magnet corresponds to the sphere of the spirit. You spoke correctly about the spheres saturated by the spirit. Only when spiritual striving leads to the realization of the nature of the dimensions of various spheres is the realization of the higher worlds affirmed. One may join in evolution limitlessly.

61. Beyond the visible, the spirit of an Agni Yogi penetrates by means of the manifested fire of the centers. Thus, the Mother of Agni Yoga can penetrate through manifest striving. Thus is the cognizance of the unseen world brought to the spirit of an Agni Yogi. Yes, yes, yes!

62. When in antiquity purgatory and fiery hell were spoken of, certainly transmutation and karma were meant. When the laws were established, their meaning was known. Exactitude of knowledge was expressed in manifestation by the Cosmic Magnet. The knowledge of karma was asserted by the luminaries. Purgatory was put in the place of karmic striving. Purgatory in its present understanding was inherited from the law of transmutation. The fiery hell followed as the law manifested by karma. Karma and transmutation are inseparable! One principle predetermines the other, and the tension of the one evokes the striving of the other. Creativeness of great attraction constructs all cosmic principles. Only striving directed to the manifestation of Fire can yield the formula of reality. Humanity in its heedlessness denies this reciprocal law. Verily, karma and transmutation outline the evolution of the spirit. Space resounds with these laws, and only the law of the Cosmic Magnet directs the striving toward evolution. A sensitive ear will catch these harmonies.

63. Karma and transmutation constitute factors which are directed toward progress; they create the effect by the propulsion of karma and they set the direction through transmutation of spirit. When the striving creativeness attracts the spirit to the Cosmic Magnet, the fiery effect is inevitable. I affirm that the law of karma and transmutation leads to consummation. The seeking spirit, being permeated by fire, is attracted to the Cosmic Magnet. When We, Brothers of Humanity, speak about the Cosmic Magnet, We perceive therein all manifestations of the higher laws. Verily, all that is most beautiful and most pure is contained in this law. Therefore, when We said that the

Cosmic Magnet brings into strain all manifestations that contain the whole beauty of Be-ness, We had in mind the saturated, the manifested Cosmic Magnet.

64. The link between the visible and invisible worlds is affirmed by the correlation with the Cosmic Magnet. As. in the entire Cosmos, the link exists as a necessity. Each energy and each element forges a link with identical energies. Likewise, the spheres are not isolated. Thus, the invisible world confirms its link with the visible one. The subtle energies penetrate into the circle delineated by the manifestation of attraction. Therefore, the Spatial Fire strives into human spheres, and the spirit strives into the invisible sphere. Thus, space reciprocally attracts the striving energies. The invisible world creates its effects. Thus, the attraction of the energies is boundless.

65. In the linking of the spheres is contained the creativeness of the Cosmic Magnet. Only attraction creates, and the Magnet impels the energies to the affirmed forms. Attraction predetermines human life. When karma propels the spirit to its destination, the Magnet creates. Thus, karma presses upon the heels of human ascent. Thus is built the manifestation of consummation. Therefore, when the spirit knows its path the Magnet acts. It is thus that the predestined is affirmed and the Cosmic Magnet acts.

66. Cosmos is built upon the affirmation manifested by attraction. Heterogeneous energies are attracted to one seed. Thus, pure fire is at the base of each cosmic combination. The cosmic creativeness is expressed in the assembling of the best combinations. Space is magnetized by the rush of the energies. Often the Cosmic Magnet unites the properties of different energies for acute shiftings. Therefore, when the Cosmic Magnet is strained, sundry imperfect forms are attracted to the seed, which works them over again. Thus the space links its forms. Therefore, when We speak of the creativeness of the Cosmic Magnet, We bear in mind the pure fire that is contained within the shell of various energies. Hence, humanity is directed by the Cosmic Magnet, but only a conscious attitude makes for progress.

67. The spirit's creativeness builds like the Cosmic Magnet. The shield of humanity lies in the spirit. Nations are moved by this lever. Only the creativeness of spirit establishes the step of ascent for humanity. Thus can evolution advance powerfully. The striving of the spirit intensifies the destinies of nations.

68. Cosmic attraction is directed toward the affirmation of all manifestations. The heart assimilates all energies directed to it. The heart expresses all strivings in life. All cosmic energies are attracted to the heart. Those who deny the conscious attraction of the heart deny the significance of the Magnet. The Spatial Fire is impelled to the heart, and in this principle is comprised the entire cosmic process. Hence, Cosmos dwells in the attraction of the heart. Only the energies based upon the attraction of the heart produce life. Thus, the life chain is endlessly forged by the heart.

69. The life-creating force of the heart is most powerful, and it may be said that it is a magnet. Thus, creativeness of the heart is the propellant to consummation. Only these attractions saturate the cosmic creativeness. Thus, the cosmic heart quivers in the Arhat. Thus, the cosmic heart quivers in the Tara. Thus, the cosmic heart quivers in the atom. When the consciousness awakens, the Chalice resounds. Therefore, Our path is paved by the heart.

70. The Absolute is not contained in a transitory form, but the spirit of the form expresses Absolute

Reason. The shell of the cosmic seed in its transmutations is subject to the law of time, but the spirit of the seed endures beyond time. Thus, the cosmic form is renewed eternally, but the substance of the striving seed depends upon the Cosmic Magnet. Thus, the beauty of Be-ness is saturated by the Cosmic Magnet. The spirit which has discerned the substance of karma aspires to liberate the seed from its encasing shells. These shells gather like mist around the seed. Each seed goes through its battle on its way to the Infinite.

71. These battles and victories are most vividly brought out by the transmutation. Only when the spirit is strained in fiery striving can the shells be transmuted. Only when the spirit strives to the pure Fire can the shells be transmuted. When the spirit of an Agni Yogi regenerates its shells, the fiery transmutation is affirmed; this is the highest process, and in its tension it embraces all cosmic spheres.

When the center of the lungs is kindled, each kindling successively strains a new current. The affirmed receptacle of fire thus correlates with the Fire of Space. That is why the centers must be so greatly protected. Before consummation the centers resound with especial subtlety. Hence, the separation from Earth makes itself very keenly felt. The heart is the receptacle of all the finest energies. The subtlest currents resound upon the heart.

72. The incompatibility between spirit and matter compresses itself like a rushing vortex. When the spirit is burdened by contacting imperfection through the shell, it begins a battle which discloses this imperfection. The shells that impede the spirit are like encumbrances obstructing the path. Truly, encumbrances! The cosmic creativity incessantly clears away strivings toward darkness. Humanity's chief lack, lack of under-

standing, lies in this expressed disharmony. When the spirit and the shells which clothe it will be in harmony, humanity will come closer to the cosmic union. Thus, when the striving to the fiery process will be assimilated a new step will be affirmed. The striving of humanity to the manifestation of imperfection is developed upon the principle of light-mindedness. Speaking of the highest harmony, it is said that Cosmos creates upon the principle of unity of life. Therefore, one may attain only through unity. Thus, the Infinite summons spirit and matter.

73. The Cosmos is strained in the blending of its parts. So powerful is the principle of blending that it may be stated that the most powerful lever is the principle of unity. Magnetization through the spirit expresses the decision of the Cosmic Will. Only the creativity of spirit can truly be called the creativity of Eternity. Thus, the creative seed of the spirit strains each striving cell. The spirit determines the chain of lives; thus, the cosmic union is so powerful. Hence, the affirmed union is constructed upon the attraction of the spirit. Yes, yes, yes! According to cosmic law the principle manifested by the spirit gathers those seeds which respond to the attraction of the Magnet.

74. In the intercourse with the projectile energies, a link of identity is outlined like that manifested between the pull of the Magnet and these energies. Each intercourse sets the foundation of a magnetic spiral, and upon this spiral the world energy is built. The fiery Agni Yogi experiences the adherence to the world spiral. All spiritual leaders of humanity feel the attraction of the world spiral and act in accordance with it. The spiritual leaders strive with the course of evolution. Hence, when intercourse with the Cosmic Magnet is established, cosmic fires are assimilated.

Therefore, when the Spatial Fire creates, the spiritual leaders penetrate into the fiery spiral. The sensitiveness of the spiritual leaders allows them to assimilate the energy of the subtle spheres, transmuting it in life. Hence, life cannot flow without these fiery streams.

75. The spiritual leaders permeate life with their essence. When the creativeness of the spirit is intensified, all missions may be fulfilled. The Cosmic Magnet creates its affirmed spiral. The affirmation of the spiral establishes the property of the fiery attraction. The cosmic blending advances along the fiery spiral. Verily, the higher sphere is being linked with the planet. Indeed, there occurs a blending with the essence of Spatial Fire. Verily, a life can be affirmed as the reflection of a cosmic ray.

76. Fire directs all processes in Cosmos. The invisible process of life is directed by the fire of spirit. Immutable is the law of fiery creativeness; in it all manifestations are contained, and it carries in itself all creative possibilities. Thus, amidst all inexplicable cosmic manifestations of Be-ness, let us seek the Fire. The inception of life and the shiftings are one and the same manifestation of Fire. The ineffable creativeness has Fire in its seed—Fire invisible, pure, creative.

77. Cosmic regenerations create new forms. Cosmic regenerations eradicate the outworn forms, evoking new ones to life. Thus, the rhythm of cosmic regenerations shifts the spatial manifestations. The afflux of new forces strains the cosmic spiral. Thus, cosmic creativeness equilibrates the shifting of forms. The dates of departing energies predicate the dates of approaching energies. Hence, the cosmic shiftings are focused upon the dates of cosmic regenerations.

78. The regeneration of the spirit is affirmed also by the eradication of old boundaries. Thus, when the creativeness of the spirit is tensed by its approach to the Cosmic Magnet, the spirit then partakes of cosmic regeneration. These regenerations comprise in themselves the entire potentiality of the spirit, and the step of regeneration will provide a new formula. Hence, when the creativeness of the fire of the spirit is strained for the construction of evolution, it gathers identical energies. Thus does the Agni Yogi gather energies for regeneration. Therefore, the flaming centers can create regenerations. Thus, the cosmic fire is assimilated by the centers.

79. The cosmic fire of life inception suffuses the affirmed manifestations upon the planet. Each impulse which lives in the energies suffused by the fire collects its own psycho-dynamics. The life-engendering fire creates, affirming the potential of the seed.

80. Each cosmic action carries in itself the impulse of Fire. The creativity is divided, going both into the physical and into the psycho-life. In psychic creativity the ray of pure fire is affirmed. The manifestation of psycho-life is so powerful that the insignificant part put into physical creation is engulfed by it. We affirm that spiritualization creates.

81. In the decisions manifested by Cosmos, the most unusual conditions coalesce; hence, a keen tension of the centers is so necessary. New conditions will provide unusual possibilities. If one considers that the new conditions will be ten times as great, the manifested possibilities will be multiplied a hundredfold. What vast constructiveness! I consider that even a mite can yield a great harvest. If only people would ponder these laws and bring at least a mite!

Parallel with the new conditions, the tension of the currents is also increasing. The increase of tensity effects at the same time many manifestations of a burning out of weak organisms. Therefore the strengthening of the human centers is so important.

82. The preciousness of life is not acknowledged by man, whereas the manifestation of life is wondrous and boundless in the possibilities for ascent of the spirit. Humanity dislikes looking into the distant future, and its consciousness stirs about in the dust of the immediate proximity. So long as humanity refuses to learn to look into the distance, it will be impossible to decrease human sufferings. The difficulty humanity has in assimilating the Fire of Space greatly retards the dates.

83. The pledge of the Teacher should be understood as an extremely scientific factor. Only upon evidence of a corresponding consciousness in a disciple can the pledge be given. The disciple can either consolidate that pledge or sever it. The strengthening of the pledge can create a powerful bond which is inseverable when the disciple's consciousness is in conformity with it. The correlation of the consciousness to the task is the fundamental condition for a mission; therefore, it is important that the disciple should manifest correlation of consciousness.

84. The search for new ways is the most imperative problem. Due to the unusualness of conditions of the future, it will be impossible to proceed by the old ways. All new ones must remember this. It is the worst thing when men do not know how to escape from the old rut. It is dreadful when people approach new conditions with their old habits. Just as it is impossible to open a present-day lock with a mediaeval key, likewise it is impossible for men with old habits to unlock the door to the future.

To all We shall say, "It is necessary, necessary, necessary, to find new ways!"

The quality of finding new ways is precious. Therefore, We test a disciple upon his ability to adjust himself to unusual conditions.

The appearance of new currents will astonish humanity. As usual, these currents will be beneficent in the hands of those who know; but in the hands of the ignorant they will be a scourge.

85. The currents proceed according to the law of least resistance. Hence, the weakest parts suffer and are burned out. Therefore, growth and strengthening are most necessary. Each retardation at the moment of tension is not only dangerous for the one who retards but is ruinous for a part of the planet.

86. If it expects success, humanity must, above all, accept the future. For there cannot be success with the past. Thus, the search for new ways is the first requirement. The evidence of flexibility in the search is the basis of success.

87. The action of the magnet at a distance is conditioned by receptivity; hence, the sensitiveness of the spirit is most important. Of course, a powerful magnet can overcome inertia, but the dissipation of power is great. Hence, sensitiveness of receptivity aids evolution, and an inert spirit retards it. With sensitiveness of receptivity, the power of the magnet can act at enormous distance.

88. Humanity must develop sensitiveness if it desires to avoid a catastrophe. How is it possible that it does not understand that help can come only if the Guiding Hand is accepted! One must point out that if the Guiding Hand is not accepted catastrophe is inevitable.

89. The mighty Magnet is acting upon the planet; the currents are now especially tense. This manifestation will mean a growth in power, and much that is

weak will be consumed. The powerful Magnet will affirm the future.

When We sound a summons for the manifestation of sensitive receptivity, the need is great. Humanity must understand that We cannot move stones. The consciousness of humanity must manifest sensitiveness.

90. A multitude of forces is acting upon the planet, and the reaction of other luminaries is only a part of these forces. Among the invisible effects, the manifestations of magnetic centers, which are constantly growing, are very powerful. These manifestations will soon be accessible to simple physical observations. Study of their power, tensity and correlation will bring a new science.

91. When the effect of the forces will multiply, humanity will become panic-stricken and chaotic in actions. Serious ailments will be on the increase.

92. Innovations in all domains of science and in the schools are indispensable. One cannot go far in the future world with the old science. On one hand, one must eliminate all the useless accumulations; on the other hand, one must penetrate more deeply into all manifestations, augmenting contemporary achievements. At present, too many years elapse before the achievements of laboratories, researches and discoveries reach the schools and the people. It will be necessary to establish information departments in schools, with popular presentation of the latest discoveries. A greater speed in communicating these informations is indispensable, because newspapers fail to give some of the most important information.

93. Broad dissemination of knowledge can regenerate the world. Knowledge can achieve miracles. Let us recall the words of the Blessed One concerning ignorance. Each success depends upon knowledge,

and if there is nonsuccess somewhere, it means that ignorance has crept in. Hence, let us say that knowledge is above all things. Where there is knowledge, there is the manifestation of beauty.

94. The pledge of the Teacher excels in beauty the evidences of correlation between the Teacher and disciple. In the East the understanding of the Teacher is valuable in that the disciple senses this beauty.

When people will accept the concept of the Teacher, a new step will be prepared. Much, much does humanity lose in failing to accept this concept. Yes, yes, yes! All new ways are thus barred to humanity, and the quests must begin with this acceptance.

95. The Teaching of the East regarding Yoga is incomprehensible to the Western mind, and the heart does not sense its beauty. Hence, the evidence of non understanding bars the approach to the future. It is essential to affirm the new approach by means of the acceptance of the concept of the Teacher.

How can one reject this most beautiful concept! And what a loss to humanity there is in the deferment of dates! The coming of threatening times will bring many to their senses and will affirm a new beginning.

96. Straight-knowledge is developed in the quest for new ways. Therefore, flexibility is the mark of straight-knowledge. Let us say to all new ones that the decisive rejection of old habits and an aspiring search are the foundations of success. People must finally understand what it is that benefits them!

97. The law of shifting creates by gathering particles which pertain to a new cosmic combination. The pull attracts all free energies to where the particles are being directed. Hence, each new step constitutes an attraction of the Cosmic Magnet. The spirit choosing its path is indeed attracted to its seed, thus consummating a cosmic and predestined path. Hence, Our law proclaims, "Strive toward the highest!"

The spirit beginning its path is permeated with Spatial Fire. Hence, when the spirit is not overburdened by life it can, in affirming its new path, manifest a new quality. Thus, under Our law new qualities are affirmed, and the Karma of humanity not only can contain the shifting but can thus be enriched by a new karma. Thus shall We conclude the exposition of karmic shiftings. In the infinite course of the spirit, let us accept the law of shiftings.

98. When a new step affirms new happiness, We manifest our Vigil. When a new step is imbued with new striving, We manifest Our help. Therefore, when I affirm a new step, the manifestation is quite apparent.

99. The tension in Cosmos is directed toward the creation of new combinations. The tension of the spirit is directed toward the construction of new steps. Only those who have adhered to Us know the power of the tension of creative labor. The mist which clouds human reason is composed of fragments produced by lack of understanding. Thus, humanity smites the planet. Whereas, substance is unlimited and in it are contained all tensions. Hence, humanity should strive toward tension.

100. Much is affirmed by Us, and tension will bring the predestined. Those who have dedicated themselves to the cosmic tension must conquer. Hence, Our world-wide victory is irrevocable. Therefore, when that which is predestined by the Brotherhood is to be fulfilled, joy resounds. Therefore, I have said it—I vouch for it! I see victory! Yes, yes, yes! During ascent the difficult hours transform failure into success. Thus, let us remember—Victory and Joy! Thus, the new step is predestined by the Cosmic Magnet.

101. The invisible sphere which surrounds humanity is being woven out of the strivings of the human spirit. When the sphere is woven, the intensified tempo of the predestined manifestation sets its course. Hence, the thoughts intensify the sphere and react upon the course of events. Thus closely bound is the affirmation of events with the cosmic course and with the tensity of thought. Space is considerably tensed by these thoughts. The downfall of countries and their rise depend upon these strata. Each striving movement toward the higher spheres evokes a higher creation. Only quality lends distinction to the tension. Only quality affords the spirit its proper change. Thus, without end, quality is being forged in Cosmos through tension.

102. You are correct in speaking of the inner growth; this lever develops an action similar to the pull of a magnet. When Our Tara manifests her self-sacrifice for the benefit of mankind, it may be said that an invisible flame is moving humanity in conformity with the Cosmos. When Our Guru in self-sacrifice submerges into the earthly spheres, it means that he is invisibly propelling the human development. Thus, humanity's growth is intensified through the invisible levers of the spirit. Hence, the growth of the works through tensity is revealed as similar to the growth of an inner magnet. Therefore, the might of the spirit is invincible.

103. Verily, in the manifestation of Our Works the foundation is set upon a new striving. Thus, a new step provides humanity with new understanding. Therefore, those who have set the foundation of cosmic tension will give humanity a new quality: that of consciously becoming cosmic co-workers. Thus will Our founded works accord one more quality to humanity,

which will bring the spirit closer to cosmic cooperation. The Cosmic Magnet acts powerfully.

104. The cosmic law does not require submission, but a conscious cooperation directed toward construction affirms the cosmic creativeness. The Spatial fire contains in itself multifold properties. The principle of cooperation should be adopted, and all those who know the principle of containment can accept this cosmic law. Hence, when the power of the spirit grows, those who know the cosmic law strive toward cooperation. Thus, let us aspire to limitless cooperation. The spirit that knows the laws can intensify all fires. Let us emphasize that one should strive toward the knowledge of Be-ness and should be strong in following the law of cooperation.

105. The participation of cosmic forces occurs through their attraction into the channels of action, during which a better combination is assembled. The creative impulse is tensed when the energies are assembled for manifestation. During construction and reconstruction various energies are attracted; thus, each driving energy impetus sets up tension, and each action is channeled by the influence of the Magnet that is drawn toward the seed of the spirit. When life demands a channel of action, the striving spirit must act through a pure channel. The channel of action must accept the formulae of the manifestation of the Magnet. Thus, quest endlessly for the channel of action.

106. Verily, the space rings with joy when the foundations of Be-ness are being proclaimed. Cosmic Right is asserted in the realization of the affirmation of cosmic law, and the joy of Be-ness fills the space. Thus, the Law of the Lords creates the current of a new life. Hence, I will say that Cosmic Right is garbed in the radiance of cosmic manifestation.

107. The perfecting of the forms is directed to the highest manifestation through the drive of the energies. The same law pertains to the striving of the spirit. The attraction of the spirit to the creative manifestation is imbued with the striving of the will. The fiery transmutation is expressed in the progress of all manifested centers. Hence, when the will of the spirit is transmuted, the law of progress acts in its spiral. This spiral progress then proceeds in all dimensions. When the spirit can complete the round of life, rising above the point of its beginning, then verily the spirit has attained the striving which will affirm it in the direction of the Cosmic Will. Thus, Cosmic Will governs each progress into the Infinite.

108. The manifestation of cooperation with Us affirms the tension of all centers. When the spiral acts, advancing toward evolution, the spirit of Our co-workers is verily strained by pure fire. When the spirit of the co-workers is imbued with pure fire, the spiral of creativity is affirmed. Thus, let us accept the law of spiral tension. We affirm that the spiral of the will carries the spirit on the wings of cooperation. Thus, We see the growth of the spiral of the spirit. Therefore, We affirm the sacred bond of the heart and rejoice when the wings of cooperation radiate in the tension of joy. Yes, yes, yes!

Thus, Our Shield proclaims: "Cosmic cooperation exerts the best possibilities."

109. When transmutation attracts the energies to a fiery creation, the striving impulse accomplishes a cosmic action. Each energy summoned for creativity is a co-worker of Cosmos. Likewise, the spirit summoned to action is confirmed as a cosmic co-worker.

What action is it that is founded upon cosmic cooperation? Each action of forward striving means a step in evolution. The evidence of forgetfulness of one's own "I" indicates adherence to evolution. The closed circle of the heart produces an oppressive formation. The Silvery Lotus that is unfolded on all sides indicates the containment of all cosmic fires. Thus is an open heart affirmed in Cosmos.

110. Yes, yes, yes! Verily a new world! The joy of the spirit provides all possibilities. When the great future is affirmed, Our creativity embraces all manifestations. When We are assembling a New Race, We intensify all achievements. Thus, this wondrous year has revealed manifold affirmations of the great future. Radiant foundations have been laid.

111. The cognition of the Cosmic Magnet will help humanity to understand all planetary perturbations. When the spirit can accept the substance of the Magnet, it can penetrate into the higher spheres. The knowledge of the law of magnetic attraction, applied to life, will provide the understanding of higher spheres.

When the Cosmic Magnet preordains a planetary manifestation, the law puts under tension all surrounding strata. When human deeds surround the planet with strata of darkness, then the Cosmic Magnet certainly asserts a corresponding manifestation. Therefore, the luminaries which surround the planet act in cooperation with the cosmic Magnet.

112. The Cosmic Magnet intensifies all human strivings. Verily, the alliances of nations are thus affirmed. Space resounds, Space calls, Space awaits.

Each spirit that is aware of the Cosmic Magnet must acknowledge the responding vibration. When striving toward this vibration will be affirmed, then the immutability of the task will be illumined by the understanding of Cosmic Consciousness.

Chance is not a symbol of affirmation; therefore,

Our close ones can sense Our Law. Thus radiant are the pages about the Cosmic Magnet!

113. Wherein, really, lies the wealth of humanity? In the construction of new steps. Spatial thought holds the tension for the creation of new worlds. Each spatial thought is man's possession. Hence, the stratifying of the space should be the paramount care of humanity. How then is it possible not to give importance to this factor? Even a simple daily formula says that the construction of a step depends upon the degree of striving. Hence, each step reflects a creative direction. Thought is dependent on the direction imparted by the spirit. Hence, the spatial thought reflects the collective thinking. Let us accept this law about spatial thought for the sake of clarification of cosmic vistas. The crumbs of thought also have their consequences. Thus, humanity must choose between pure striving and spatial contagion.

The path to the Infinite lies through a perfect consciousness.

114. The wealth of humanity consists in spirit-creativeness. The principle of cumulation lies in spirit-creativeness. The principle of striving lives in spirit-creativeness. Therefore, the Cosmic Magnet can be sensed through the spirit-creativeness. The growth of spirit-creativeness in man is affirmed by the cumulation of the Chalice. The Cosmic Magnet knows the guiding power. The pledge of the future lies in spirit-creativeness. Yes, yes, yes! Therefore, We vouch for the impelling force of Our actions. Thus, that which was founded by Us will give new dates to the world. Therefore, the predestined will come. The Crown of Existence radiates with all cosmic fires. Thus, life for an Arhat is variegated as the radiation of the cosmic fires. Yes, yes, yes!

115. The organization of cosmic courses is affirmed by various cosmic combinations. The power of the main course issues from the seed of the manifested magnet of attraction, evidenced as the foundation of cohesion. The seed of the spirit is that magnet which collects all energies that are being inrooted. Therefore, the potential of the spirit is most fully expressed in action. The seed of the spirit and action constitute the center of life. Action, issuing from the potential of the spirit, is predetermined by the accumulation of the Chalice; hence the link between the cause and the effect. The quality of tension must conform with the quality of action. Especially important is the harmonization of the effect with the growth of tension. Hence, the potential of the spirit proceeds in parallel with the quality of tension.

116. Humanity has given great emphasis to the concept of Guardian Angels. When thought can sense the proximity of a spirit from other spheres, why not accept the Image of the One who guides the destiny? When humanity will realize His power, it will cognize the significance of the true Guardians. The Guardian of Spirit, the Guardian of Truth, is the One who directs our steps into the Cosmic Space. Man can think about Guardians. Thus, a spirit close to Us can sense the Guardians in the Cosmic Space. Hence, creativeness of the spirit brings one to the close Guardians. Thus, let the strivings to the Guardians be maintained upon all paths. Sensitive receptivity affords striving to the Guardians.

117. Cosmic shiftings are always followed by an increase of new tensions. Each shifting brings in its wake a strained spiral. Hence, each shifting predicates a multi-faceted manifestation. States which yield to the law of cosmic forces and shiftings intensify the affirmation of their strivings. Thus, the law of shifting brings into strain diverse sectors. Nothing remains unaffected in Cosmos, and everything is mutually intensified. The creativeness of spirit is similarly strained by varied strivings. The shifting of consciousness carries one onto the path of evolution. The improvement of life upon the planet depends so greatly upon the shifting of consciousness that progress will be expressed chiefly in the direction of thought. Hence, humanity's greatest care lies in the progress of thought. When the guiding rudder will be understood it will be possible to join in the creation of cosmic matter.

118. The great purpose in Our actions is to aid humanity in the shiftings of consciousness. Our disciples are appointed as such helpers. Each shifting of thought produces its effect. Therefore, Our mission is to lead human consciousness into a shifting, and the mission of Our disciples is to set the pace with the Cosmic Magnet. Our Stronghold contains the essence of the shifting of the consciousness and the directing of it toward the center of evolution. Hence, the shifting of thought is the paramount healer of mankind.

119. Each action is strained by the lever of spirit and the lever of heart. Cosmic creativeness expresses forms by these levers. In Cosmos, the lever of the spirit is the consciousness of Materia Lucida, and the lever of the heart is the same manifested symbol of attraction. How greatly humanity has deviated from the great principle of the creative Magnet! Man has accepted the center of the creative impulse as his Ego, and the action of the Ego absorbs all tensions. Thus, instead of a cosmic action there results a focus of egotism. The creativeness of Cosmos evokes cooperation. The creativeness of Cosmos evokes striving to the far-off worlds. The focal point of the Ego, rejecting all ordinances of Cosmos, generates causes which affirm the manifestation of isolation. Cosmos attracts dates which are identical with the direction of the Cosmic Magnet. The core of the Ego proceeds in isolation. The creativeness of Cosmos manifests boundless cooperation.

120. The attainment of a spiritual step can direct humanity to the source of Truth. Only by way of tension and by way of striving may one progress toward evolution. The visible world brings to humanity a concept of the invisible one, and the creativeness of spirit can direct toward cognizance of the invisible. The creativeness of spirit can reach the highest summits. Hence, when the cosmic tension is invisibly transmitted to man, We call it cooperation with the Cosmic Magnet. Spirit-creativeness is attained by cooperation with the Cosmic Magnet. When the spirit verily realizes the tension and direction of the Cosmic Magnet, it is able to build the steps of ascent.

121. The achievement of the spirit is great when the fires are being transmuted. The law of transmutation draws in its wake every striving. As an eternal teacher the spirit strains all possibilities. The fiery transmutation not only affirms the subjection of the lower to the higher but also draws the highest striving from the substance of the spirit. Therefore, when the spirit verily decides to renounce its encumbrances it opens the way to transmutation. Therefore, the disciples must remember that transmutation is granted only when the spirit has conquered selfhood. Selfhood is the progenitor of all grayish encumbrances. Hence, when the manifestation of egotism thus obscures the spirit, it can be stated that the fire of transmutation cannot contact it. Thus let everyone remember!

122. The responding foundation is abundantly manifest in cosmic construction. Each energy has its

own responding vibration, and the predetermining force depends upon the vibration of receptivity of the energy, which establishes perfection of form. The same law is at work in human constructiveness; thus, the responding vibration is established by the principle of attraction. The principle of responding vibration is inlaid in the responsibilities of humanity. Having lost subtleness of receptivity, humanity has lost subtlety of the senses. The responding vibration is inaccessible to such a coarse man. Therefore, since the striving toward responding vibration is inscribed upon Our Shield, one must perceive the way to responsibility. Let us conclude with a call for sensitiveness.

123. The feeling of responsibility is truly most powerful. The Lords carry this mighty key to the General Good. Spheres of various tensions are charged with sensitiveness of energies. The tensions of varying tasks manifest the responsibility, and the spirit which reveals the sensitiveness of responsibility deserves affirmation. Thus, Our Tara carries the responsibility for the progress of human thinking, and she offers her experiment for its regeneration. Thus the Guru establishes the evolutionary movement. I affirm that those who carry the responding vibration in the Chalice will provide a new step.

124. Advancement toward evolution predicates the tension of all centers. All progress of peoples depends upon the striving of the centers. Humanity has constructed its steps upon nonacceptance of the law of the centers and of the true tensions. The ascent of the spirit is tensed by the highest centers. Therefore, movement into evolution can be manifested only when the spirit has realized the greatness of Fire. Manifestations of Fire and of the centers will give a new science to humanity. The creativeness of the heart is strained by the center of the Chalice. Thus, the progress of the manifestations of Fire depends upon the tensity of spirit and the accumulations of the Chalice. Having surrounded its established world with thorns, humanity has indeed lost its way. Thus, the manifestation of Our Teaching will give the wings to humanity and open the path to Infinity.

125. When the spirit surrounds its own power in the seed by an accumulation of encumbrances, it renounces its striving. So burdensome are the encumbrances that the spirit loses access to the Towers. Hence, those who come to know this advance only through transmutation of the Ego. When the spirit cannot push itself to root out its encumbrances, it piles up solid obstacles. A balance is maintained between the striving and its result. Thus, the wings of the spirit provide the power of flight into the higher spheres, but the weight of a burden marks the steps of him who strides to the lower spheres.

126. During communion with the far-off worlds one must accept the degree of Fire. The fire of purification explains all the ancient mysteries. When Christ spoke of the spirit needing regeneration, He had in mind the fiery purification. When the outline of the law of The Wheel of Life was given by the Lord Buddha, the fiery purification was affirmed. Thus, the consuming of old encumbrances is affirmed by the fiery purification. The new ascent is conditioned by the purification through Fire. Therefore, the purification of spirit lies at the basis of transmutation. The highest Agni Yogi is not an instrument nor a passive recipient but a co-worker and creator. Therefore, when the fires of Cosmos are strained the manifestation of fiery purification is inevitable. Thus shall we establish attunement with the fiery purification.

127. The great law of purification acts through the affirmation of transmutation. When the spirit of an Agni Yogi approaches Spatial Fire, the creative centers are tensed. Therefore, when the tension of the Chalice is great, the creative manifestation is fiery. Thus, the center of the Chalice creates.

128. When the Cosmic Magnet brings together the particles destined to coalesce, all obstacles are dissolved by the power of the attraction. Hence, the overcoming of obstacles leads to the predestined. The currents of the Cosmic Magnet are immutable. Verily, the sacred Magnet is the power of Be-ness.

Upon each field, upon each action, upon each manifestation, the cosmic blending radiates. Each vibration is strained by the pull of the Magnet. Therefore, the Sacred Action lives in every cosmic manifestation.

129. The Sacred Action of the Cosmic Magnet preordains all creative moves in the Name of Maitreya. Only by this sign will you conquer. Therefore, when Our Might affirms the step, the stone of foundation lies firmly. The manifestation of obstacles lies as the path of consummation. Cosmic action is tensed under the sign of unity; thus, We ascend through the mighty Magnet.

130. In Cosmos there is a law which foresees all the best combinations. Does not the law of attraction move the striving particles? Is not the law of gravitation put in effect by the Highest Reason? When people speak about harmonization they penetrate very little into the essence of the law itself. Cosmic creativeness contains in itself the substance of the great Materia Matrix. Attraction is a property established for the expansion of Cosmos. Therefore, this law acts upon all planes, in spirit and in matter. The foundation of construction is established upon the manifestation of the better possibilities, and the creativity of spirit proceeds under the same mighty law. Hence, while the creativeness of Cosmos is put in tension by sundry factors, it should be understood that the main impulse is given by the Highest Reason. Thus is the Infinite built. Thus is the world chain built. Thus is Cosmos built.

131. Who can respond to the beauty of cosmic creation? Who can sense the Highest and resound to all pure manifestations of Cosmos? We shall say that it is he who carries within himself all the highest fires. I affirm that only the vibrations of the finest energies can disclose the higher spheres. Therefore, the Bearer of the Chalice upon the earthly plane is proclaiming the Cosmic Right. The spirit that has realized the purity of the creative fire can become a forceful leader. Therefore, he who carries the Silvery Lotus in his Chalice awakens through his vibrations the accumulations in others. The creativeness of the white ray is replaced by the radiance of the Silvery Lotus. Thus, the magnet of the spirit verily leads the striving ones to attainment.

132. Each striving spirit is attracted to its foundation. The manifestation of karmic ties is founded upon attraction. The attraction to the foundation affirmed by the Cosmic Magnet is intensified by the impulse of creative fire; it is thus in each element, each atom, each spirit. The Cosmic Magnet tenses each karmic attraction; hence, all vital relations create karmic conditions. The karmic conditions are being built upon the principle of attraction; and when the creativeness of life is understood but little the karmic attraction assumes very ordinary dimensions. Hence, when the progress of a spirit is in step with the Cosmic Magnet, the Cosmic Magnet leads the affirmed spirit to its foundation. Thus, the spiritual tie attracts the spirits closest to each other. This law is immutable.

133. The karmic law affirms all vital rights and governs all karmic attractions. Thus, the property of the Cosmic Magnet is laid into each karmic foundation. The manifestation of life indicates the development of polarity. The manifestation of a potential of attraction evokes receptivity in a close spirit. Thus, the indicated and existing laws will effect the preordained. All planes have their karmic laws.

134. The Spatial Fire purifies the earthly crust. Pure emanations approaching the earthly sphere rarefy the dense emanations. The acceptance of Agni Yoga will confirm humanity in its conscious communion with the Cosmic Magnet. The communion with the Fire of Space will afford possibility for amelioration of earthly conditions. The creativeness of Cosmos affirms the cooperation of all spheres. The Spatial Fire decreases the pressure of the gases upon the earthly sphere. Therefore it is affirmed that the attraction of the Fire of Space will bestow a better step upon humanity. The conditions will improve when the centers will awaken.

135. The sensitiveness of an Agni Yogi purifies in the same way the layers of accumulations with his fires. The fiery concept can bring out all the higher functions of an Agni Yogi. Only the fire purifies and creates. All the higher manifestations are intensified by Fire; furthermore, the date approaches when Fire will be raging. Only a new step, defining the turning point of humanity toward the new manifestation, can be given for this decisive and affirmed epoch. Hence, since the decisive battle before the advent of the Epoch of Maitreya has been sanctioned, a fiery experiment is being placed before humanity.

136. The true spiritualization leads the spirit to the fiery purification. Each striving directed to the fiery purification is confirmed by a higher impulse. When the vital impulse directs man to manifest, the centers lead him to spirit-creativeness. Besides this, the spirit gains illumination of the Ego through the tension of Fire. Each surging energy is aware of its path, consciously obeying the law of attraction. The fiery transmutation gives the most subtle understanding of the significance of the Cosmic Fire and discloses its creative essence. Therefore, the knowledge of the fiery transmutation attracts the spirit to the path of limitless illumination. Thus the great work of Fire proceeds.

137. The spirit who sacrifices himself to affirm the great principles of the cosmic fires brings to humanity a lofty step of illumination. Thus, each Lord brought the Light of the cosmic fires. Because of these rays humanity lives, and evolution advances by these steps. The Fire of Space removes the unapplied affirmations. The spirit who sacrifices himself for the benefit of evolution bestows his radiant Lotus on humanity. Only the highest Agni Yogi knows the path of illumination, and the directed fires are manifested to humanity as the beacons of salvation. Yes, yes, yes! Thus, Our Mother of Agni Yoga gives the fiery salvation to humanity. Thus, the Guru provides the fiery urge toward Beauty. I confirm the co-workers striving to the fiery transmutation.

138. A great life is confirmed by the manifestation of the Cosmic Magnet. Three planes are manifested to humanity for the affirmation of all principles. Indeed, it is easy for the spirit to strive upon the higher planes, but the earthly, the lowest pole, is established as the place of decision. Only there where Light and darkness battle can the spirit manifest a free choice. Imbued by the emanations of the energies, the spirit can establish itself through the expression of its striving. Only when immersed in the earthly sphere can one manifest the

subtlety of striving into higher spheres. Cosmic creativeness requires entirety of manifestation. Thus, the spirit composed of all cosmic energies must pass through all cosmic steps.

Verily, man must pass through purgatory; otherwise, the spirit cannot attain the predestined world, which comprises all spheres.

139. Only in spheres where a shadow veils the vision can the spirit seek the Light. Only where the shadow stands behind its back can the spirit display its strength. Only where the shadow conceals the far-off worlds can the spirit reveal its power of discrimination. Therefore, the growth of the spirit is quickened through obstacles. Hence, Agni Yoga is given as the loftiest and most direct path. The knowledge of transmutation will reveal all possibilities. Therefore, when the fiery experiment is confirmed for humanity its offering will be unlimited.

140. Humanity is saturated with cravings. When the spirit yields to the asserted cravings, the step into evolution is limited by the visible. The opposite striving of the spirit establishes the step of affirmed evolution. The two opposites are always mutually confirmed. While one part strives to possess the visible, the other part strives toward the invisible. Thus, in an epoch of cosmic reaction, humanity may be divided into slaves and those who strive for cosmic cooperation. The planet is populated by slaves to possession and by those who carry the cosmic fires. Thus, Our Carriers of Fire do battle, and the clutching hands are of the slaves bereft of spirit. Only those striving to Infinity can understand the beauty of Be-ness.

141. If it is possible to confirm the segment of the cosmic fires which is already accepted by humanity, then why not admit the growth of those manifested fires? Since the spirit is subject to changes under the influence of various physical manifestations, why not acknowledge those which take place under the influence of the spirit? I affirm that the spirit transmutes all qualities and harmonizes all tensions. The transmutation of the centers is tensified by the fire of the spirit, and the creativeness of the centers is focused on the assimilation of the higher fires. As the manifested vessel, the heart admits the currents of all the most subtle energies. Thus, the harmonized currents are absorbed by the all-containing Chalice. Hence, the currents absorbed by the center of the Chalice correspond to the higher energies; and the transmission of the psychic energy are accompanied by reverberations. The higher tension corresponds to the higher fires. Thus, the spirit creates unceasingly.

142. Upon the cosmic scales there are manifested two main causes, which uphold the cosmic organization. Each cause predicates the reorganization of the world. The effects of the cosmic causes are strained according to the substance. Thus, upon the cosmic scales rests the evolution of the world and its dark opposition. When the world is being reorganized, the dark side creates impediments. Let us see how the forces for the accomplishment of world tasks are affirmed across the span of millennia. When the Carriers of Light affirmed the manifestation of the Covenant, the potentiality of their striving was infused into the spirit of humanity. When the striving of despotic conquerors was asserted under the law of egotism, man sank into a sphere of restrictions, and darkness propelled him toward self-destruction. Hence, the self-renunciation of the Lords flamingly leads humanity. It is the principle of self-destruction that brings on a new step of evolution. Thus is the path of the world cleared. Over and above all consequences radiates achievement, and the path of self-destruction leads to the lower spheres. Thus, even darkness affirms the step of Light.

143. The spirit striving to self-assertion through unlawful means takes a heavy karma upon himself. Unlawful usurpation constitutes a burdensome step. Therefore, let the consciousness grow toward absorption of the designated cooperation. When conceit stifles the most elementary concepts, how is it then possible to attain the understanding of the Teacher? The creativeness of spirit is inconceivable without the principle of Hierarchy.

144. The magnetization of the space proceeds by means of manifold attractions of fire. The rays of the luminaries are most powerfully affirmed attractions. Besides these forces, magnetization is maintained by mutual attraction. Therefore, the property of magnetization progresses through reciprocal creativity. Thus, in Cosmos all energies create by reciprocal magnetization. The striving and the receiving energies are dependent upon the potentiality of the attraction; and when the affinity is great the combination will be pure. Thus, a receptive spirit imparts to the energy the quality of striving. Only the property of magnetization produces the effect. Therefore, the boundless path is illumined by the power of magnetization.

145. Human accumulations create a network which encircles humanity with a manifested web of denials. This concretely established net of denials acts as an impenetrable covering. The net is punctured by arrows from similar spheres. The spheres which surround the planet are formed in this way. The creativity of Cosmos depends so greatly on the attraction of identical energies that all formations are confirmed under the

law of attraction. The law of Light is so powerful that the transmutation of the rays brings into tension the necessary currents. Thus, Light engulfs the darkness, and the network which surrounds our planet can be dispersed by the current of rays. The stroke of the rays upon the dark covering sets up the rhythm of Cosmos. The steps of evolution are built upon this rhythm. Thus, the world is manifesting an upheaval, and the cosmic energy stands ready to enter into the course of the world rhythm.

146. When the spirit sinks into the darkness of denial he cuts off all links. Karma acts so precipitantly that the process of redemption sets in under the law of the Cosmic Magnet. Therefore, when the spirit builds his steps of ascent the declarations of denial have to be eliminated.

147. The realization of an attraction tenses the spirit striving to the principle of Fire. When the spirit touches the fiery principle, it is imbued with the power of the Cosmic Magnet. Each contact with the fiery threads effects a link with the higher worlds. Only the principle of consciousness can impart the beauty of the higher worlds. When We speak of the higher worlds, an understanding of every subtlety must be manifested. Creativeness untiringly attracts all the higher elements for perfecting. Thus, the spirit can strive toward the evolution into perfection. When the spirit-understanding will begin to draw in the subtle elements, it will then be possible to manifest to humanity the symbol of true Be-ness. Thus let us build the path to Infinity.

148. Of all principles leading to the broadening of consciousness, the principle of Hierarchy is the most powerful. Each manifested change is based upon it. Whither can the spirit direct itself without the Guiding Hand? Where can the eye and the heart turn without Hierarchy, when the Giving Hand of the Hierarch affirms the flow of destiny, and when the Hand of the Hierarch directs one to the best manifested date, and one becomes familiar with even the highest energies? Therefore, the seed of the spirit becomes imbued with the Cosmic Ray of the Hierarch. Since the most powerful principle contains in itself the potentiality of fire, the pure Fire of the spirit of the Hierarch is affirmed as the highest principle. Thus shall we remember our spiritual Leaders. Thus shall we revere the Law of Hierarchy.

149. It is most difficult for humanity to accept the law of the Cosmic Magnet because it is difficult for the spirit to get accustomed to the path of universal energy. The fluctuations of the spirit create a peculiar track, and instead of universal striving the spirit writes the page of the visible only.

When a man is attracted by the Cosmic Magnet, all universal laws support this choice of the spirit. Hence, attachment to the Cosmic Magnet separates the spirit from the narrow understanding of the Ego. Thus, the circle drawn by the Cosmic Magnet establishes life upon the principle of General Good. Only the higher striving leads to universal energy. The urge of personal cravings does not bring one to the universal energy. Only the realization of the Cosmic Magnet will reveal the path to Infinity.

150. The essence of the Cosmic Magnet transmutes all strivings. Only the realization of attraction effects a complete karmic bond. The principle of attraction obliges one to strive. Hence, the spirit who knows his karmic bond saturates his striving with beauty. Thus, the spirit striving to union carries out a cosmic ordinance. The cosmic blending is saturated with pure fire.

The creativeness of Cosmos confirms the law of consummation. Thus summons the law.

151. Transmutation is based on independent action. The spirit which feels all cosmic tensions strives to assimilate the currents. The transmutation depends upon the striving of the spirit to attunement. Only cosmic tension can draw the spirit toward transmutation. Only the spirit who understands the power of attraction creates harmony. Therefore, when the tensed magnet of the spirit manifests independent action, the center of the Chalice fulfills its cosmic ordainment. Thus, a sensitive spirit responds to the resonances of the cosmic currents. Therefore, when the transmutation is strained into effect by independent action the center of the Chalice resounds. The creativeness of the spirit is based on the creativeness of Fire.

152. The center of the Chalice gathers all creative threads. Therefore, each cosmic vibration resounds within the Chalice. The spirit must give evidence of many indispensable strivings in order to assimilate the responding vibrations. When the center of the Chalice can manifest all the resounding vibrations of the cosmic fires, the creativeness of independent action is truly great. Therefore, this center must be protected by a moderator. Hence, it is necessary to guard the health.

The magnetic currents are greatly strained. The manifestation is strained toward the shifting of the planetary centers. The reorganization of the world is at hand; therefore, one can feel the nearness of Our hour.

153. The basis of attraction is under strain in all vital manifestations. Therefore, when life creates its steps, one may affirm the principle of this basis. Of all bases, the strongest one is Fire. Of all bases the heaviest one is limitation in selfhood. Under the symbol

of Fire all principles are united. Under the symbol of limitation a small circle of consciousness is drawn. Life collects the universal energy through the creative fires. Humanity has been endowed with manifold threads of the universal energy, but only through fiery attraction can life, as the basis, construct. Thus resounds the great base of Be-ness.

154. How greatly the contrary mind of man shrinks its foundation by severing itself from the base of universal energy! Each one who limits himself bears the evidence of severance from the Cosmic Magnet. Only the principle which manifests the unity of universal energy can create life. Therefore, every straining leads to harmonization if the universal energy lies at its base. When the shifting is so great, cosmic centers are about to become aflame. Our seeds lie at the base of universal energy. Thus, the fiery foundations affirm the Epoch of Maitreya.

155. When the creative rhythm strikes Earth, naturally the opposition is intensified. Each luminary is so powerful that its rays reach Earth. Each cosmic manifestation evokes opposition from the energies. During world reorganization, cosmic striving is transmitted to humanity. Therefore, two cosmic courses are so vividly manifested. The guidance of the Origin of Light attracts all the necessary elements. The guarantee lies in the Cosmic Magnet. The direction of opposition is seen in the urge to destruction. Thus, the guarantee of the Cosmic Magnet builds the future.

156. When the cosmic creativeness is tensed, the idea of reorganization is asserted. Hence, each creative effort encounters a pressure. Therefore, each striving has its opposition. Thus, Our tasks are in step with the Cosmic Magnet. Our Covenants build the future. Therefore We say, "Maitreya creates through the Cosmic Magnet." Thus, all opposition leads to victory. Verily, when My Spirit manifests a magnet identical to Earth's, victory can be affirmed. Let us remember the doubled magnet!

157. Whence emanates the striving to the Cosmic Magnet? A correlation of energies is but confirmed by attraction. Whence emanates heterogeneity and the attraction of dissimilar energies? The affirmation of forms can result only from the fact of differing properties. Only when heterogeneous properties are drawn into the creation does a true cosmic manifestation take place. Only when the force of polarity is asserted does the force of attraction act. Thus, upon all planes the affirmed polarities are asserted. The spirit which serves independently attracts the force of the Cosmic Magnet. The formulation of thought attracts the needed evolution. The participation of the heart brings a constructive vibration. Thus, the foundation of creativeness is the awakening of the vibration of the heart.

158. It is not the manifestations of insensibility that can sustain the Cosmos! It is not measures of passivity that can create! It is not encasement in a single shell that can build! Therefore, I say that only the key of the heart and the achievement of self-sacrifice make life out of a vibration. Only the striving to independent action can develop the sensitiveness of receptivity. Therefore, the spirit imbued with quest can ascend. Only the vibration of the heart creates. One can create only through the vibration of the heart. The greatest power lies in the magnet of the heart. Through it we seek, through it we create, through it we find, through it we attract. Thus let us remember; thus I affirm. The magnetic vibration has molded all creative manifestations. Thus, Our close co-workers, having accepted

the beauty of the Teaching, will be strengthened by the magnetic vibration.

159. Karma gathers the currents which are adapted to the affirmed improvement. When the spirit strains all efforts, the manifestation of the transmutation can develop the best possibilities. Only the adaptability to the karmic current provides the affirmed cosmic foundation. Thus, karma and striving give to humanity the essential impulses. Only the guidance of karma carries one to the step of Be-ness. Therefore, when man realizes the power of karma and strives to express the best aspirations, his path is parallel with the universal energy. The universal energy attracts the creative strivings. The future and the Infinite are thus being built.

160. The karma of misunderstood missions burdens one heavily. When the mission is affirmed as a striving toward Light, then the manifestation of striving is marked as under the law of the Magnet. Therefore, those who have understood the significance of karma can be affirmed by Our Pledge. All who have accepted the foundations of karma can act in conformity. Only the Pledge which has been cognized can cover all strivings. Thus, the karma which leads to the highest worlds is the highest step.

161. The reorganization of the world stirs up multifold rushing vortices. Each reorganization evokes the strokes of the cosmic rhythms. The rhythm of The Wheel of Life is so powerful that resistance to it cannot be asserted. The cosmic whirl intensifies all oppositions but the power of Reason engulfs the forces generated by opposition. Thus, the obstacles are swept away by the rhythm of cosmic whirls.

162. The reorganization of the world strains all forces of the dark ones. Each wave of evolution strains the forces of stagnant intent. When the world is divided into Light and dark forces, is it possible that the affirmed resultants will not be born? The cosmic creativeness is intensified through battle, and the battle proceeds upon all planes. Therefore, the manifestations which are closest to Us show themselves first of all as forces which stimulate opposition. Therefore I say, "The predestined will be fulfilled, the preordained will be fulfilled." One should preserve the joy of the future; one should affirm victory!

163. The principle of shifting is determined by the Cosmic Magnet. Each change activates new energies, and each spatial thought generates a new possibility. Therefore, when the shifting is confirmed by departing forces, their end verily can be foreseen. Thus, before the rise of the New Race the old foundations crumble. Each departing race therefore strenuously resists the assault. Thus are the cosmic shiftings created.

164. The impulse of the departing forces calls up innumerable identical currents from space. The manifestation of the approaching change greatly strains all the lower strata. For the affirmation of the predestined, a striving spiral must be created. Therefore, the New Race is assembled under the sign of victory. The step of manifested consummation is strained by the approach of the appointed date.

165. The violation of the balance affects all planetary manifestations. An energy which has violated the cosmic balance sets up a different direction. The link between the energies is determined by the law of attraction. Therefore, every energy that responds to a new striving generates life through its corresponding attraction. Thus, events and spatial manifestations are so closely interrelated. Our creative impulse is intensified by the same fiery energies. When the luminaries have determined an affirmed page for a country, all energies are active. Thus, the creation of a limitless path is intensified by Cosmic Fire.

166. When imbalance takes on the impetus for explosion, all plans of the dark ones crumble. The imminent explosion puts under strain all the schemes of those who have fear. Therefore, the departing ones exert themselves strenuously.

167. The date of the shifting tenses all fires. The fire of thought is attracted toward reorganization. The fire of the spirit strains unassimilated energies. The fire of the heart strains the spheres of indignation which are striving to the power of reorganization. Therefore, when the creativity of Cosmos encounters hindrances, a new channel is created. Hence, Our Brothers forge with the Cosmic Magnet. You will conquer only with Us!

168. With what does humanity enshroud the Earth? The most opaque sphere is that of egotism. The most worthless sphere is that manifested by the worm of jealousy. The most destructive sphere is that manifested by conceit. These spheres destroy families, empires, churches and all kinds of organizations. Whereas, Cosmos summons to cooperation. The approaching change can sweep away the human accumulations, but each participant in these accumulations carries the karma of the planet. The human creativeness is reduced to destruction. The spirit striving to Infinity participates in cosmic cooperation.

169. How is the concept of peace apprehended in the human consciousness? The foundations are false and are manifested as the affirmation of a willful direction. When the Lord said that He brought to Earth not peace but the sword, none understood this great truth. The purification of the spirit by fire is that sword!

Can purification be accomplished without striking blows? Is it possible to purify the striving without annihilating the dross? Is it possible to manifest achievement without striving of the spirit? Only the sword which smites egotism can link the spirit to the higher world. The one who rests upon a false peace verily builds self-destruction. Thus, the word of the Lord about the sword furnishes the symbol of purification.

170. How resounding are the words of the heart about hidden motives! How important it is to realize impartially the intentions of the spirit! Three traits of character will help to cognize the potentiality of motive; the trait of honesty, the trait of self-abnegation, and the trait of service. The manifestation of each trait will give the spirit the sword against egotism. Not the hand of karmic tension but the hand of self-exertion will hold for the spirit that gleaming sword. Let us remember that fire which gives tension to the motive. Let the spirit of egotism thus approach the fiery transmutation. The Tara points out the path of fiery self-exertion. The Guru points out the path of fiery action. Yes, yes, yes!

171. The cosmic shifting creates a strenuous conflux. The cosmic stroke creates an impetus which is unrestrainable. Hence, the torrent called forth by events manifests the response of masses. To the call of the Cosmic Magnet manifold reverberating spheres respond. Thus, when the call of the Cosmic Magnet strains forth, the tension of masses leads to transformation. The creativeness of the Magnet attracts all strivings.

172. A very precise application of the defined sword of the spirit can raze the dams. When a fiery thought tenses the spirit, the attraction of various energies is inevitable. The sword of the spirit smites and creates; the sword of the spirit collects and cleaves the imperfect manifestations; the sword of the spirit is tensely poised by the Cosmic Magnet.

173. The flaming sword of the spirit is the basis of multifold fiery manifestations. The creativeness of an Agni Yogi contains the potentiality of these energies. The creativeness of the spirit contains these energies. Therefore, I affirm the great process of creativeness of the spirit of the Mother of Agni Yoga. We reverence the transfiguring fire of the spirit. The fire of the centers thus creates. The Lord has ordained the manifestation of the fiery torrent. Thus is the sacred heritage manifested in life.

174. Concordance between forces is needed for a cosmic combination. Only when human consciousness can sense a cosmic vibration can a form be affirmed. All predestined cosmic combinations exist in space and the human consciousness must penetrate into the subtlest energies. Every thought is generated from contact with the reservoir of space. Thus, the most immediate task of man is to awaken his consciousness to the significance of cooperation with the Cosmic Magnet.

175. Only when the consciousness adopts the course of the Cosmic Magnet will it be possible to affirm the predestined. Only when man understands the direction of the Magnet will it be possible to affirm a new step. Thus, when We direct to a new step the course of the nations is drawn taut by the Cosmic Magnet. Verily, the epoch of purification approaches! The Cosmic Magnet creates the future. Therefore, the shifting is inevitable and only a broadened consciousness can keep in pace with it, having assimilated all creative perturbations. Thus, all tensified currents create a new step. Thus, a manifestation of urgency grips the countries. The strivings toward construction

and toward destruction balance the planet. Thus, the impelling force of Our actions proceeds with the Cosmic Magnet.

176. When man became a plaything of destiny, he himself had chosen his fate. When man became subjugated to the yearning for possession, his egotism obscured his development. Man indeed has become the slave of the dark forces; therefore, the sword of purification is imperative. The development of consciousness strains all centers. Striving is awakened at the approach of the sword of purification.

177. The cosmic construction is under strain; therefore, the tension of the nations is so irrepressible. Each country is like a chord in the cosmic creativity. As the subterranean fire continuously links the centers, so do the events link the countries. Under the pressure of the Cosmic Magnet, all nations now show stress. With the approach of catastrophe people sense the force of the shifting. It is a very serious time; events are being generated. Thus, the tension of the time can create a new step. It is a very difficult time. Darkness always veils the horizon before the dawn.

178. Nations fashion their destinies upon the principle of independent action. Each country builds its principles around its seed. Thus each country acts, straining different energies. Creativeness which lacks the higher principles produces a karma of destruction. Parasites which suck all the sap from the trees bring the karma of extermination upon themselves. Hence, when Our law proclaims cooperation, it must be realized that without this principle the better step cannot be created.

179. When the nations create a new future, the energies are assembled by the power of the spirit. When the power strives to establish the Cosmic Right, the departing power tightens its snares. A difficult time manifests always new possibilities. Hence, the Cosmic Right is creating its channels.

180. Each cosmic form is determined by its karmic tension. When the element of fire destroys a manifestation on the planet, it means that this place must be regenerated by fire. When the element of water submerges some land, it means that this place had to be purified. Thus, a cosmic shifting must strain into action new spheres. Of course, the human records should be carefully verified, because human deeds bring man to his fate. The planetary karma is impelled by the element of fire, the element of thought, and human deeds. Thus, We are propelling humanity to a better step.

181. When a new karma approaches, a better step in the progress of evolution is affirmed. All new steps have been affirmed as an ascent. Only the human hand threatens the affirmation manifested by Cosmos. Only the human hand works in opposition to its predestination. Therefore, the striving to regeneration should be the motive power of the nations. Verily, under our own eyes shiftings are affirmed. Thus, Light smites the darkness. I so affirm!

182. The nations are seeking the manifestation of the cosmic fires. Only cosmic striving provides the necessary formula. Only cosmic tension provides the necessary formula. Therefore, when these forces in the nations are seeking manifestation, the consciousness is impelled toward the Cosmic Magnet. Thus does evolution mold its steps. The steps of ascent are tautened by the Cosmic Magnet. Whoever opposes the Cosmic Magnet makes a contrary wave. Thus, when striving to the Cosmic Magnet increases, the step toward evolution is approaching.

183. In Cosmos every perturbation predicates a chain of perturbations to follow, each one creating a next step. Therefore, the nations must set forward under declaration of striving. The time is very serious. Cosmic shiftings enter into power; hence, Light battles with darkness. Therefore, when the forces of nations are strained, the sparks of the spirit create like the sparks of a conflagration. Thus, every sensitive spirit senses the shifting.

184. The cosmic energies are strained into blending by the driving Fire. Each life pulsation carries in itself sparks of Fire. Each striving life pulsation is marked by the Cosmic Magnet. So also, thought is strained into pulsation by Fire. So many errant thoughts fill the space! Space vibrates with thoughts. A thought vibrates by a current of spirit, and it may be said that their manifestation prognosticates the cosmic creativeness. Thus, all prognosticating thoughts must vibrate with the fire of spirit. A thought deprived of the vibration of the spirit manifests deathliness. Only the vibration of the spirit can create.

185. How majestic is the law of the vibration of the heart! How majestic is the law of unity! How majestic is the law of spirit and consciousness! Therefore, when the force of unity is asserted, the opposing forces become tense. The manifestation of Light approaches. The predestined will be fulfilled. So I affirm!

186. The striving of the spirit intensifies the courage, imbuing man with the energy of fire. The power of will gives man the most aspiring and harmonious step to beauty. Only during manifestation of the constructiveness of spirit is a form a beauty brought forth. Hence, when the power of courage strains the creativeness, the result is in conformity with beauty. Let us say that only in coordination with the Cosmic Magnet can a form of beauty be created. Thus, each movement of people which is intensified by the power of spirit affords a new step of evolution. Therefore, the beauty of tension corresponds to the beauty of the creativity of the Magnet. All cosmic ordainments correspond with beauty. Thus, the path to the Infinite summons to beauty!

187. He who walks with the Brothers of Humanity cannot merge into the mist of uncertainty. He who walks with the Brothers of Humanity is under tension through the power of the Cosmic Magnet. He who walks with the Brothers of Humanity crosses the boundaries by unknown ways. He who walks with the Brothers of Humanity is tense with the courage of the spirit. He who walks with the Brothers of Humanity carries within his spirit an invulnerable sword and in his aura a resistant net. Thus, let us remember. Many hostile arrows has My Hand broken! A perpetual and unmitigating struggle strains the impulse of life. Thus the battle progresses, and the departing forces strain their efforts toward destruction.

188. Straight-knowledge intensifies all the highest manifestations. Only when a being of man expresses straight-knowledge is the pledge affirmed. When the sensitiveness of the spirit utilizes all energies sent by the consciousness through a center, when the spirit can receive the resonance of Cosmos, then verily can straight-knowledge be affirmed. An Agni Yogi kindles the torches of sensitive spirits.

189. The sensitiveness of receptivity of an Agni Yogi is most subtle; it expresses the most refined response. The subtlety of straight-knowledge impels the spirit to the higher spheres. As if providing wings, the straight-knowledge exalts the spirit. The spirit of the Agni Yogi strives forward like a predestined fiery

stream. Therefore, Our Mother of Agni Yoga fierily creates. In the Epoch of Maitreya each fiery attainment is reached through tension; hence, each striving action has fire in its essence. Thus, Our closest co-workers create fierily. When We say "fierily" it means ardently; it means by the higher ways; it means in pure spirit; it means through beauty; it means through the understanding of the Common Good and, having understood the Common Good, it means without self-interest, without egotism; it means by applying the Teaching.

190. The sensitiveness of the spirit is strained toward a questing for communion with cosmic manifestations. The being imbued with the quest for communion with the higher spheres is striving toward cosmic ordinances. Every energy is drawn taut by the lever of Fire. For humanity, this lever is the basis of the creativeness of spirit. When the spirit in its striving senses the ordinance of Cosmos, it fulfills the law of Cosmic Reason. How vividly the fiery Agni Yogi expresses communion with the higher spheres! The spirit of the Fire-Carrier knows the power of communion; therefore, when the universal energy approaches, the fiery spirit knows the date. The ordinance of the Cosmic Reason imbues the spirit with sensitiveness and transmits to it each cosmic move. The sensitive spirit sets up a fiery current with the higher spheres. Let the fiery torrent take the place of oppressive immobility.

191. The fiery torrent penetrates all spheres. The fiery spirit penetrates all spheres. Therefore, when at the head of an undertaking there stands a fiery spirit, victory is assured. Each ordinance of Fire is transmitted by the fiery spirit. Therefore, the fiery path knows the affirmation of Cosmos.

192. The law of containment is affirmed by all

beginnings. When the cosmic creativeness is brought into strain by aspirations, the law of containment brings forth manifold formulae. In cosmic creativeness the treasury contains all manifestations of energies. In spiritual creativeness the Chalice becomes filled with the very same energies. Hence, the treasury of the spirit has to contain all energies. Thus, the law of containment governs the essential creative impulse. From the Chalice issue all creative laws and in the Chalice are gathered all cosmic manifestations. Therefore, the enrichment of the Chalice affords realization of all cosmic plans. The foundations are gathered in the Chalice, and each energy can be a creator. Thus, creativeness is molded by the law of containment.

193. The spirit who has assimilated all concepts is freed from the thrall of prejudices. The spirit who has assimilated the concept of Common Good embraces all manifestations of human needs. He who has assimilated the concept of the Cosmic Magnet can intensify his creative impulse. Thus, Our co-workers must realize how immutable is the path of striving toward the Brotherhood. Since Our affirmations are blended with the Cosmic Magnet, the Brotherhood exercises all laws. Thus, Our affirmed law of cooperation is intensified by the Cosmic Magnet.

194. The regeneration of the nations succeeds their decline in consciousness. Each country passes through these steps. The creativeness of consciousness strives toward regeneration; therefore, the most precise indication of a shifting will be the regeneration of consciousness. Thus, each step of a people's consciousness is reflected in either the downfall or the progress of a nation. Therefore, an impetuous awakening shows the potentiality of the nation's spirit.

195. The achievements of yesterday bring on the

day of the future. Where the soil is teeming with the emanations of labor, a harvest may be expected. Thus, the soil of Our works is teeming with the seedlings of great beginnings. When the soil is saturated with creativeness, the seed must bring forth its fruit. Therefore, I affirm the future. The spirit creates most fierily.

196. The Chalice which embraces cosmic manifestations is saturated with cosmic energies. The Spatial Fire which strives to take form awakens the saturated Chalice by attracting the Fire of Cosmos. Thus, each visible form is built by the creativeness of the Chalice, and the Silvery Lotus proclaims the manifestation of all-containment. All cosmic manifestations have their response. Therefore, when the Chalice contains all fires the spirit knows Be-ness and the Silvery Lotus knows cosmic creativeness. Thus, the all-containing Chalice resounds in Infinity.

197. Cosmic vibration impels humanity toward the Spatial Fire. When the thought undergoes shifting, then the Fire of Space contacts this thought. One must understand the tension of that thought which, as a driving fire, penetrates everywhere. The evidence of Spatial Fire should be discerned in all manifestations. All records of Spatial Fire carry cosmic vibrations with them. Hence, when humanity will understand the might of Fire the responsive vibration will be easily affirmed, and human creativeness will develop in fiery construction. Thus, cosmic creativeness is strained limitlessly by the Fire of Space.

198. The accumulation of the Chalice responds to the cosmic vibration. If humanity would come to know the tension of the Spatial Fire, verily it would be possible for humanity to gain the knowledge of Agni Yoga. Now, when small sparks are within the understanding, the approach of Cosmic Fire can be revealed. The magnet of the Chalice is so powerful that the evoked vibrations create.

199. The vibration of the heart expands like a magnetic wave of spirit. The vibration of the heart expands like a ray of light. In all cosmic manifestations, the Magnet of the Perfect Heart attracts. Only the lever of the heart can direct the action toward the true source. When the ray of consciousness contacts the Spatial Fire, the cosmic vibration enters into life. Therefore, the conscious direction of the ray of the heart will lead to creation. Thus, the cosmic attraction is imbued by the Heart of Cosmos. When the vibration of the heart strives to create, the energy of the Cosmic Magnet responds to that striving. Thus, conscious attraction will produce a boundless striving.

200. The vibration of the heart draws the spirit toward its destination and tenses all the levers which attract the spirit to that which is determined. Therefore, when creativeness is impelled to the manifestation of consummation, the heart resounds. Each vibratory striving thus affirms a response, and the ray sends a corresponding vibration. Therefore, the sensitiveness of the heart affords assimilation of the rays that are sent. Certainly, when a concord of vibrations is established the ray does not cause fatigue. Thus, one may say that identicalness effects harmony. I so affirm.

201. The substance of the spirit is manifested in striving. The Chalice in tension affirms the straining of the spirit. All threads which issue from the Chalice lead to action which is linked with the Spatial Fire. It can be said that the creativeness of the Chalice links the Spatial Fire with the accumulations of the Chalice. Only the circle of consciousness will impart striving to creativeness. Thus, Our law proclaims affirmation of the Chalice. Each vibration attracts invisibly the Spatial Fire, and the sensitiveness of the spirit strains the sparks of the Chalice.

202. The sensitiveness of the spirit of a flaming Agni Yogi gives impulse toward the Cosmic Magnet. Since We have sent to the planet a new affirmation of Fire, it means the time is drawing near.

203. Humanity prevents the cosmic forces from penetrating into the orbit of the planet. Every energy of Cosmos is attracted by the Cosmic Magnet, but its assimilation depends upon humanity. Only consciousness can attract toward constructiveness. Therefore, when the human spirit is on the step of denial the forces of Cosmos cannot manifest themselves. Thus, creativeness is generated by human consciousness. Only the spirit-creativeness focuses all cosmic possibilities, and the lever of the heart sets the direction of the spirit. The consciousness which responds to cosmic attraction creates the forms of psycho-life. The manifestation of striving to the realization of a responding vibration indicates the responsibility of the spirit. Only in fearlessness before Infinity, does the spirit realize the very purpose of Be-ness.

204. When the Magnet alerts identical parts, the purpose of its attraction is a harmonious blending. When We unite arcs of consciousness, the circle is completed. Thus, a cosmic action unites all the identical energies, and an attraction between the arcs is asserted. Long ago I pointed out the creativeness of the Magnet. Thus, let us remember the great Cosmic Law.

205. Humanity ponders little upon the source of creativeness. All outer manifestations are accepted by humanity as ordinary. The Spatial Fire outlines definite functions. But behind the departing energies stands the source of the inexhaustible cosmic energy. About this invisible and all-pervading source humanity

should ponder. Each creative thought must be directed to this source. The chain of causes and effects must be discerned in all cosmic labor. This chain is boundless in all dimensions.

206. The chain of causes and effects strains the fiery lives. As a rushing torrent, the fiery consciousness awakens the creative impulse. The chain of causes and effects strains the fiery centers. Therefore, the manifested processes are drawn near by the Cosmic Magnet. That is why the centers vibrate so greatly and the rays are reflected upon the heart.

207. When the spirit is able to strive to the understanding of the purpose of Existence, the torrent of creativity of Our Brotherhood can be shown. When We strive to establish equilibrium, We point to the Cosmic Magnet. Supremacy will not be established where domination is being expressed, nor where the asserted domination is creating its channels, but there where the forces of evolution are being assembled; not where the striving is directed toward selfhood, but there where creative steps are built in the name of the Common Good. Thus, humanity creates its karma.

208. Verily, all laws are contained in the consciousness. Only the all-containing consciousness can create forms and assert new lives. The all-containing consciousness attracts the knowledge of cosmic laws. The all-containing consciousness affirms that each form is bringing a response into evidence. Only the all-containing consciousness creates through all cosmic centers. The consciousness which holds a saturation of cosmic fires presents a correspondent manifestation. We encompass adherence to the Cosmic Magnet; and only then may it be said that the spirit is living in space. All striving energies bring into manifestation other corresponding energies. Thus, the spirit which contains the power of the Cosmic Magnet builds evolution.

209. The creativeness of the spirit of the all-containing Agni Yogi strives to the higher worlds. Consciousness gives the key to cosmic energies. The consciousness of an Agni Yogi strives toward accord with the Cosmic Magnet. The creativeness of the centers vibrates to all cosmic manifestations.

210. The consciousness that embraces the cosmic centers affirms the full Chalice. The consciousness that embraces the principle of Fire will give to humanity new possibilities. The spirit strives to the Cosmic Magnet without disconnecting its chain. The attraction to the seed of the foundation is verily an attribute of the fiery spirit. The consciousness of Infinity in Cosmos gives a fiery ray.

211. Only that consciousness which strives to the Cosmic Magnet can understand the power of the coming change. Only a time of grave significance can bring such forces into play. Hence, there is tension throughout the entire Cosmos, and in the highest tension is the shield of the future forged. Therefore, the moment of reorganization attracts new possibilities.

212. The rays of space penetrate into the seed and intensify the potentiality of the spirit; only by this impulse can the spirit create. When the potential of the spirit comes in touch with the ray of Cosmos, the spirit-creativeness is asserted. Thus, each form is generated by the spirit and the cosmic ray. How little people ponder over the grandeur of creativeness! How little understood is the thought which is tensed by the cosmic ray! How little understood is the Cosmic Might in all its manifestations! When humanity will understand that creativeness comprises cosmic seeds, it will assimilate the cosmic rays.

213. The fire of the centers is a most powerful and conscious force. When the strained centers sense a cosmic shifting, they create with Cosmos. Therefore, the creativeness of the spirit is so powerful, and each conscious tension evokes a response.

214. The saturation of space is most serious, and major importance must be given to the quality of saturation. When the space is encumbered by manifestations of non-striving energies, dark clouds of failure are suspended. Each thought impressed on the space generates its own coloring. Therefore, the area around each action is saturated by the quality of thought. Each thought generates its stamp and responds to the immutability of the impulse. Faith in the immutability of the Cosmic Magnet must imbue the space. Cosmic shifting will be a direct result of the Spatial Fire, and the spirit who understands the responsibility for thought will strain the spheres with pure fire. The more tense, the more pure. Thus is the creativeness of the Cosmic Magnet built.

215. How powerfully the spirit of the Agni Yogi creates! So many strivings are affirmed by the Carrier of pure Fire! So many possibilities are awakened! Each pure thought creates an apparent zone of light in space. Like a purifying fire burns the pure thought of an Agni Yogi. Into this zone various cosmic rays are attracted. Hence, space has its rainbow-like zones. Thus does the pure fire of an Agni Yogi create.

216. The substance of the cosmic fires is directed by the Cosmic Magnet. There where the Magnet pulls, the cosmic fires are drawn. The space strains the fires in the direction of the Magnet. Therefore, the significance of the attraction lies in the direction of the fires. Each thought in the space attracts the creativeness of the fires. It is to be affirmed that humanity must attain

the striving toward the cosmic fires; then the epoch of cosmic energies will approach. On this realization depends the approach of evolution.

217. The centers of an Agni Yogi increase the assimilation of fires which will bring knowledge to mankind. Hence, the centers create with the current of evolution. Therefore, the centers of a striving Agni Yogi serve the Common Good. When the Chalice is filled with fire, the aura attracts the force of the Magnet. The power of the centers must be acknowledged. Thus, the centers spiritually create, and the fiery creativeness shifts the consciousness of humanity.

218. If humanity could only learn that the separation of spheres leads to the destruction of a most powerful principle—world cooperation! All cosmic spheres are bound with one and the same principle; thus, the impulse of Fire saturates all spheres.

Only cosmic isolation can impel to destruction. Therefore, when humanity will understand that the whole cosmos breathes by the one impulse it will be possible to bring nearer the new energy. Thus are the new steps of evolution laid.

219. How important it is to realize the binding thread between the spheres! The subtlety of receptivity of an Agni Yogi is that binding thread. Upon this thread is cosmic cooperation built. The Spatial Fire and the centers create in harmony; therefore, each energy strains the centers.

220. When the shifting of the countries is being affirmed, all energies are strained. As threads, all the tensed forces are gathered and the various strivings are forged; hence, every spatial thought alarms the adversary. Each thread has its defined boundary, and each force has its orbit. Thus, cosmic thought which is woven from the vibrations of the Cosmic Mag-

net forces the invincibility of action. The demolition of energies contrary to evolution is saturated with self-destructive opposition. Thus, limitless creativeness proceeds above the destruction.

221. When striving leads toward the Cosmic Magnet, the course of the spirit is imbued with Fire. The so-called errant strivings create so much destructive karma! When the spirit breaks its karma into parts directed to different spheres instead of utilizing the channel directed by the Magnet, this spirit must pass through many steps. When the direction is in line with the Cosmic Magnet, the striving proceeds by the steps of evolution. Thus, the nations which are in step with the Cosmic Magnet approach the higher striving.

222. When the spirit shifts its accumulations, its striving draws it toward the asserted Magnet. Therefore, every tension of the centers is calling forth a new cosmic combination. The creativeness of the centers calls forth an intensified energy. Therefore, all independent action of the centers is imbued with Fire, and the flame of the spirit kindles the impulses of those who surround it; therefore, one must co-measure in expending the psychic energy. It must suffice for all things; hence, the strength must be guarded. One should not fatigue oneself after sunset.

223. The correlation of cosmic transformations is called cosmic creativeness. When Cosmos shifts the forces, the balance of the spheres is disturbed. When the balance of these forces is upset, forces in the space are drawn into a new tension. Thus, when Cosmos shifts, all spheres are shaken. Indeed, all forces expand in response to an attraction, and the cosmic harmony is intensified by the Cosmic Magnet.

Thus is Infinity created.

224. The creativeness of the spirit is intensified

by the forces of the Cosmic Magnet. The creativeness of the spirit embraces all saturated fires. The shifting is strained by the might of the spirit. Only the spirit tensed by the Cosmic Magnet can assert its highest possibility upon Earth. Only when there is receptivity can one manifest the tension; only then can one strive into a shifting of cosmic forces. Our entrusted ones manifest this receptivity.

225. The accumulations around the planet are so very dense that it is difficult for the rays to penetrate this mass. Therefore, the spatial ray can contact only those who have rarefied the sphere by their striving. The spirit, by straining its aura, attracts the cosmic rays from the space. Thus, records are borne in space in these attractions of the cosmic rays. The spirit who has rarefied the cumulations about him proceeds forcefully toward evolution. Thus, those attractions which are saturated by striving are tensed by the Cosmic Magnet.

226. The creative impulse impels the spirit to the Cosmic Magnet. The creative impulse gives birth to all strivings. The creative impulse evokes from space the manifestations of cosmic rays. Certainly, only a fiery spirit can tense all the forces needed for creativity. The creative centers of an Agni Yogi collect the rays of free energies, and therefore the fire of the centers creates currents of striving. Thus, the striving attracts the cosmic rays. Thus, We affirm the Chalice of the Agni Yogi to be a mighty treasury.

227. Gathering cosmic energies, the Cosmic Magnet develops the creativity of the Fire. Each energy attracts its own currents. Thus, a lack of coordination between spirit and matter brings on a striving for transformation. In this transformation is comprised the entire cosmic reality. Therefore, when a spirit is

tensed in a true quest he attracts new possibilities. Thus, limitless is the creativeness of Cosmos.

228. A spirit who transforms consciousnesses is called a creator of man. Only when Our Carrier of Fire calls into play these tensions does the proceeding along with Us attract new possibilities.

229. Vibrations of the tensed force of the Cosmic Magnet reach the energies of striving. The manifestation of striving attracts all vital energies. Therefore, when We elect for an achievement, We gather all striving spirits. The creativeness of the spirit is greatly strained. When the cosmic fires draw one into the vibrations of the Cosmic Magnet, the fire of striving strains the spirit into creativity. Hence, when the Cosmic Magnet determines the step of ascent, the Cosmic Magnet strains all levers. Thus, the spirit of the Agni Yogi carries in itself the impelling force of the fires, and the course of evolution is directed by the fire of spirit.

230. When thought attracts from the space a driving manifestation of Fire, the Cosmic Magnet tenses the spirit. All Lords walked under the guidance of the tensed Magnet. Only an intense Bearer of the General Good directs the fires to achievement. That is why the striving Agni Yogi is so tensed. In Cosmos the manifestations of a fiery spirit is immutable. Therefore, when Our Envoy walk in tension new steps of evolution are being laid. Therefore, the centers must be carefully guarded. Great steps are being laid.

231. Much is spoken about cosmic creativeness, but understood is only the finite creativity that is in the various manifestations intensified by the elements. The chief thing is overlooked: that the cosmic seed is spiritualized by the higher energies. But when the creations of Cosmos are straining forth, the attracted sparks of intensified fire are seeking the vital fire. Only

Fire creates spiritually, and the cornerstone is the eternal law of attraction. Therefore, the necessary energies are intensified into fusion by an irresistible attraction. Therefore, it may be said that the cosmic creativeness depends on the impellent force of Fire. In Cosmos, there has never been an affirmation that did not respond to attraction without destruction following.

232. Along with the work of cosmic creativity, that of shifting proceeds. Only an intensified consciousness can encompass the knowledge of these shiftings. It is necessary to harken to the growth of cosmic actions in order to understand the entire cosmic tension. Only where the cosmic creativeness is tense can one feel the great shifting. This grave time carries the picture of the future. The key lies in this cosmic shifting. The cosmic constructiveness is tensed by the Cosmic Magnet.

233. When We speak of cosmic energies, We direct the thought into the higher spheres. Creativity depends on eternal activity. Cosmic creativity lies not only in the combinations alone but in the striving of the vital impulse. The major action of the Cosmic Magnet consists in manifesting the vital impulse. Therefore, when the consciousness acts upon the impellent force of Fire, it may be affirmed that the vital impulse is heightened by the vibrations of the spirit. Creativeness lies not in saturation but in tension.

234. In the vital impulse of the spirit lies the entire guaranty of spirit-creativeness. In it is contained the entire fire of the spirit, which intensifies all lives. Therefore, Our affirmed law proclaims that the fire of the spirit is immutable. The creativeness of spirit thus contains all attractions within itself.

235. All the strivings of the fiery manifestations of the spirit are affirmed in the shoreless ocean of life imbued by Fire. Only when the consciousness of the creativeness of space penetrates into the cosmic striving does the Cosmos accept these strivings. Therefore, consciousness is created by attraction to the fiery Source. The symbol of the constructiveness of the strained Magnet is asserted as the great and eternal law of attraction. Thus, the shoreless ocean is imbued by fiery tension.

236. Only when the spirit adheres to the creativity of the Cosmic Magnet is it capable of aspiration toward creation; only then are possibilities drawn to it. Only when a straining spirit bears an affirmed world task does it create intensively. Constructive striving always evokes opposition; hence, there are such battles under Our Shield. But victory is inscribed upon Our Shield.

237. Each constructed step requires a new affirmation. In each formulated decision one should try to establish a new consciousness, because, for life, a molded accomplishment must be imbued with new cosmic combinations. The asserted potential calls to life the impulse of a new correlation, but the imbued seed of the spirit must find new striving. Therefore, when We say that the construction of a form reaches the vital impulse, it means that only in the development of consciousness and the forces of attraction does it reach the very essence of life. Only eternal motion gives life to all forms.

238. The spirit imbued by fiery striving manifests a drawing power for all vital impulses. As each energy reaches its identical element, so also the spirit of the higher Agni Yogi reaches the hearts of those striving to Truth. Thus, each energy of the heart molds people. The lever of the heart sets all the strained strivings. This is why people are attracted to the fiery heart of an Agni Yogi. Thus, the power of the heart affirms the manifested striving of an Agni Yogi. The creativeness of the heart can bring the pledge of Light. I so affirm!

239. The assertion of the invisible world must penetrate into earthly consciousness. The cosmic creativeness draws its creations out of the invisible spheres. When the source of creativeness is tense, the impulse of consciousness affirms the foundation of the form. One must consciously consider the source of all conceptions. Only recognition of the invisible world will afford a knowledge of cosmic manifestations. Only acceptance of the Fire of Space in all its manifestations will bring the understanding of the Primary Source. Only the invisible world contains all the intense energies. All cosmic tensions are contained in the treasury of Space.

240. When the spirit strives to an intense creativity, it communes with the source manifested by the Cosmic Magnet. When the consciousness is accustomed to flights into the higher spheres it assimilates multifold vital impulses. When the spirit is impelled by the law of attraction a current is set that is in communication with the Spatial Fire. Thus, the spirit of an Agni Yogi is strained by the consciousness of Fire.

241. Fiery creativeness is laid at the base of each entity. Even the primitive consciousness had the understanding of fire. The potency of fire is established as the measuring rod of progress. Each race has assimilated the creative fire, and the potency of its creativeness has depended upon the awakened consciousness. Thus, each race affirmed the step of its development. Fire is the impetus of life, the impetus of creativeness, the impetus of striving. Each conscious striving imparts to the spirit a cognizance of its potentiality. Each manifested spatial thought gives consciousness to the spirit. Therefore, when Cosmos sends to humanity its gifts, the link between the Magnet and the spirit is asserted. Sensitiveness of receptivity gives to everyone the possibility of adhering to cosmic creativity.

242. When Fire is assimilated by an Agni Yogi, We say that the heart absorbs silvery threads. When We point out the beauty of the Fire assimilated by an Agni Yogi, We are indicating a heart that absorbs all these threads. When We point out a consciousness that has assimilated the straight-knowledge of an Agni Yogi, We point to an immutable striving. Therefore, We pronounce the name of an Agni Yogi. Thus, the Agni Yogi will lay a bridge to the higher worlds.

243. The constructivity of Cosmos is intensified by the attraction of the Cosmic Magnet. Creativeness collects the tense elements which strive to the asserted attraction. Each basic thought carrying Spatial Fire produces a form affirmed by the Magnet. But creativeness is not contained in mere saturation. The chief thing is the vital impulse, which generates cosmic formulae. Each plan lives only by the vital impulse, and contentment brings on the manifestation of destruction. Therefore, one may affirm that the intense quest results in creativity. When the Cosmic Magnet strains all forces, a creative chain is established. Thus, the Infinite is strained toward manifestation under the impetus of Fire.

244. When the fire of spirit tenses the rays of the Chalice, various strivings are drawn to the seed. The attraction of the cosmic fires draws in threads of fiery synthesis. An Agni Yogi knows when it is best to attract the fires from the space, and the centers of attraction respond to the vibrations of the Chalice. Therefore, the straight-knowledge of a tensed Agni Yogi has the key to the cognition of events.

245. Harmony creates a forceful current. This

forceful current results in a combination which has identity. In a harmonized combination, the tensed force of the Magnet is saturated with the pull of energies. Therefore, each harmonized form bears within itself a wondrous flame of attraction. Thus, when the Cosmic Magnet strains its forces, the Spatial Fire responds with vibrations. The principle of response to the call of the Magnet creates a cosmic striving. The call and the response intensify all cosmic currents.

246. The tension of a striving spirit attracts corresponding vibrations. Only the attraction of the heart creates; and the Agni Yogi, tensed by the Cosmic Magnet, creates through his heart. Thus, when self-sacrifice of the spirit strains the spheres, the tension of impelled forces puts into strain the forces of the surrounding spheres. Therefore, when the rays of Fire contact the centers of an Agni Yogi, each center sends forth a fiery torrent.

247. The cosmic foundation is known to be the magnet of striving. The entire cosmic structure is based on the force of striving; and each step is tensed by a magnet of Fire. The Spatial Fire creates all worlds. The spark expands into a fiery sphere, and all cosmic origins increase in fiery scope, encompassing all aspirations. Thus, the spirit conceived in fire is suffused with the Cosmic Fire. Therefore, the seed of the spirit is saturated with fiery striving.

248. In Our actions, when the spirit begins to create, the predestined nears fulfillment. But the striving to the predestined encounters many obstacles. Knowing the law of the Cosmic Magnet, and of tension, We repeat about enemies and obstacles. The Blessed One decreed joy, and we ascend by obstacles. Thus, the proceeding battle strains forth new possibilities. Thus, Our Way is immutable.

249. So greatly strained is the condition of the planet that the subterranean gases are beginning to erupt. The spiritual condition is so low that the superterranean sphere is in a corresponding convulsion. The discharge of these currents only attracts tensed fires, but the densified currents engendered by humanity are so powerful that the battle of the spheres is enormous. Thus, when the world is in convulsion the battle between Light and darkness is most intense. When the shifting of the gases takes place, the Cosmic Fire is intensified. Therefore, all energies of the White Forces are strained. Verily, the battle for Truth is ratified. Thus, limitlessly, the power of Cosmos proclaims Light.

250. When Our constructiveness is brought into tension, all cosmic forces create. Light engulfs darkness. Our constructiveness is strained cosmically. Therefore, Our constructiveness proceeds abreast with evolution. Verily, We act through the intensified Magnet.

251. The dates depend upon the luminaries. The rays of the strained luminaries direct the cosmic shifting. The variety of combinations brings striving into the construction. Each shifting has its affirmed guaranty. Thus, when the dates approach, the cosmic rays give impetus to the consciousness. Thus, when a shifting brings the events into tensity, the cosmic tension creates in conformity. When Cosmos calls to a new affirmation, the Magnet unites with the luminaries. Thus, the oneness in Cosmos strains all currents and ceaselessly creates in Infinity.

252. Cosmos strains all centers and transmutes all fires. Only the pull of consciousness affords independent action. Only independent action is in step with the Cosmic Magnet, and the creativeness of the spirit, which effects the designated step, produces striving. Therefore, when manifold cosmic forces shift, the centers of an Agni Yogi magnetize the spatial thought. When the forces of Cosmos proceed to shift, the cosmic tension reacts upon the sensitive organism of an Agni Yogi. When the streams of the spirit flow creatively, the sensitive organism responds. Vast is the creativeness of the spirit.

253. The energies are strained into combination by mutual attraction. Only attraction to the basis of the seed produces cosmic combination. All kinds of energies are intensified by the vibrations of Fire, and a spirit imbued by an attraction is responding to harmony. Thus, the Cosmic Magnet gathers correlations. Each cosmic structure is imbued with fiery energies. Verily, all cosmic forms contain in themselves the essence of Fire. Boundless is the constructiveness of Cosmos!

254. The entire cosmic creation is built upon the law of striving. The entire structure is maintained upon cosmic attraction. All the consequences engendered by humanity construct their own spheres. Therefore, when Our tensions evoke currents of constructivity, the strain brings into focus currents of identity.

255. The condition of our planet is determined by human deeds. The manifestation of Spatial Fire creates spheres around the planet which protect it from suffocation. The fiery attraction is so powerful that it can be likened to a magnetic manifestation. Thus, when the forces of Cosmos drive toward a shifting, saturation of the space proceeds by the assertion of the Magnet. The planet is unable to separate itself from the Cosmic Magnet, and the chain of strivings toward the construction of evolution inseverably links all worlds. Thus, all actions of cosmic forces create in powerful

cosmic coordination, and all worlds serve the law of unity. Therefore, humanity must include itself in this law!

256. When the shifting impels all forces into action, Cosmos invariably attracts all forces necessary for the future. Only thus is each new step constructed. Therefore, when striving saturates the affirmed manifestation, the shifting takes place. All forces grow by attraction of the Cosmic Magnet. All affirmations that aspire to Us are attracted to new possibilities. Thus, the forces of Cosmos proceed in step with Our Fire.

257. The consciousness of humanity cannot be affirmed upon the visible world. Accepting correlation as a main cause in the visible and invisible worlds, one can disclose spheres of cosmic concordance. But humanity bases results upon the visible; therefore, it is difficult for the spirit to aspire to the higher spheres. Every striving spirit knows that the separation of the worlds can arrest evolution, because where the link between the Primary Source and life is severed, there one must expect destruction. Cosmic creativity is based upon eternal unification.

258. The self-sacrifice of an Agni Yogi lies in the creative impulse and in the offering of his strivings toward the manifestation of the higher energies. Therefore, when the spirit of an Agni Yogi strives toward transmutation, We say: "Since basically transmutation is directed toward purification of the space, the spirit verily is evincing a most fundamental quality."

259. The spirit which dwells upon the sphere of the visible world is thus renouncing the manifestation of the higher spheres. When the spirit lives in a realization of the oneness of the entire Cosmos, he is then linked to the entire Cosmos. Creativeness of the spirit is sustained not from without but through the striving

of the seed to the communion with the Cosmic Magnet and the Spatial Fire. The seed of the spirit knows all laws of creation; and the spirit aware of its essence seeks the link with higher spheres. The immutability of oneness impels the entire Cosmos. Verily, the consciousness reaches the most subtle energies, but the impulse which has attained striving must emanate from the seed. Thus, the key to attainments is contained in independent action.

260. The independent action of an Agni Yogi opens all possibilities. Penetrating into higher spheres, the spirit carries there its strivings. The creativeness of the spirit is intensified by the principle of interchange. Thus, each energy is coordinated in Cosmos. The tensed magnet of the spirit creates with all levers.

261. Only an intense creativeness gives results. Only a strained spiral yields motion Only a rebounding blow gives a conscious impetus. When Light battles with darkness, the strained spiral attracts all vibrations to the foundation. During all cosmic creative processes the strained spiral sets up the striving toward the Magnet. The incompatibility of the dark forces impels toward destruction. Verily, the shifting builds its towers upon the foundation of the Cosmic Magnet. Thus, the shifting perpetually replaces the departing forces.

262. Only the attraction of Our Towers affirms victory. Only the command of the Cosmic Magnet carries affirmation. Therefore, the departing forces so greatly fear Us. Verily, the manifested battle is great and all cosmic energies are in tension. Thus, We create fierily.

263. In the World Community all spiritual impulses are acutely expressed. Thus, Our affirmed Source expresses the equilibrium of the Cosmic Magnet. The World Community is perverted by humanity, and instead of cooperation humanity establishes power by domination. The creativity of humanity produces only encumbrances. Therefore, an indestructible path is laid. The Brothers of Humanity, who bring help to mankind, verily imbue the space with the creativeness of Fire.

264. The Brothers of Humanity bear within themselves the striving to save the planet. Every vital impulse dwells in the Heart of an Arhat. The urge of the Cosmic Magnet is felt by the Heart of an Arhat. The Heart of an Arhat knows the flux of the rays of the luminaries. The Heart of an Arhat knows the striving toward consummation. Therefore, Our threads flow in tension with the striving for unification.

265. Science is penetrating into the cosmic spheres and putting man in direct connection with the Cosmic Magnet. When the basis of creativeness of the cosmic fires is being denied, each manifestation of striving must be understood as an assertion of the vital impulse. Science is bringing man to the mastery of Spatial Fire, and all strivings toward the discovery of cosmic correlations are bringing cosmic power to humanity. Therefore, science must illumine the consciousness and affirm humanity in the Infinite.

266. Every consciousness that rejects the cosmic fires imbues the space with darkness. But the tensed Agni Yogi maintains the equilibrium. Therefore, the creativeness of the Chalice strains all energies. All threads of the Cosmic Magnet penetrate into the Chalice; therefore, all the centers of the Agni Yogi are under strain.

267. The element of Fire attracts all energies toward creation. When a striving creative thought imbues the space and the Cosmic Fire intensifies the creativeness of the thought, the forms then attain life. When the

purpose of existence takes on its due significance, it will be possible to endow humanity with the Spatial Fire. When existence will be established upon a higher step, the realization of the Cosmic Magnet can be affirmed. Thus, each step of evolution carries its own new energy. Verily, the consciousness of humanity is developed in conformity with the forces of Cosmos. But the will of man pre-determines each step. Thus does humanity forge its cosmic boundaries, because the awareness of an attraction can create a sphere for it.

268. Every universal thought impels the consciousness to creativity. Like fire, it reaches the consciousness of many; therefore, each such thought of Our co-workers directs the Spatial Fire into the shifting. Only in tension is victory attained. Therefore, all forces are strained and multifold mighty levers are acting.

269. When an impelled current manifests the Cosmic Magnet to humanity, the link with the Cosmos is affirmed. Thus, in mutual attraction the cosmic current can approach man. Only the independent action of man brings him closer to the Source. Therefore, each such impulse of man brings him to a higher creativeness, wherein the Spatial Fire asserts itself. Thus, when the spirit strains upward it penetrates into all spheres.

270. I feel how strained are the centers and the heart. I know how difficult it is. The tension of the centers is connected with the cosmic fires and the Cosmic Magnet. Like a magnetic needle, the heart responds to the events. Therefore, one must cautiously await. An Arhat knows the full power of invisible creativity.

271. Each spirit acquires tension under the powerful impulse of faith. Only this impulse gives man the possibility of penetrating into the higher spheres. And before cognizance the spirit must be filled with striving. Hence, when a man is straining forward upon the basis of an intensified impulse, the law of pure faith directs him to Truth. In the entire cosmic creation, the law of faith governs all beginnings. The faith of a scientist, the faith of the votaries of General Good, the faith of the disciple of the Lords, and the faith of the Lords—these are all-imbuing and are themselves imbued by the pure Fire of Space. Thus is cosmic striving created.

272. Powerful faith attracts all possibilities. Only if the lever of the heart intensifies the flow of creativity, only if the current is intensified, is the link with the Magnet established. Therefore, faith to the end will give all possibilities.

273. The lack of commensurability of humanity sets up the alleged barriers. Each instance of incommensurateness forces a current which obstructs the path to Truth. Each stoppage sets up its consequences, and this creates fetters on the manifested ascent. Therefore, one must intensify all thoughts for the General Good, and the path of commensurateness will become the path of evolution for the spirit.

274. The commensurateness in undertakings approved by Us attracts new possibilities. Therefore, each sweeping wave brings another step of affirmation. Thus, the shifting of a country proceeds on the principle of commensurateness. When the departing energies of a country are used for destruction, We affirm the gravity of the time.

275. The great law of harmony moves the entire Cosmos. When the forces unite in conscious creativity, the cosmic striving brings into tension all sparks of the Spatial Fire. Creativeness, moved by the Cosmic Will, is strained by the power of the Perfect Heart. But where the Perfect Heart is not perceived, there is no construction. Verily, construction by the Will of the

Perfect Heart affirms evolution. Therefore, only the cosmically affirmed law of the Heart lives in Infinity.

276. Each striving thought creates in the space. Each striving thought creates forms. How, then, is it possible to understand the spiritual process if the process of self-renunciation is not adopted? In the spiritual process the same principle acts, and the spirit which screens itself by the process of selfhood does not see the true Light. Therefore, the defined path to the beauty of Service proceeds by the striving of self-sacrifice.

277. The tension of the cosmic fires draws streaming particles to Earth. The records of Space are intensified by the fiery vibrations. The creativity of Cosmos is dependent upon these fiery vibrations. Thus, the spirit creates by fiery vibrations. Therefore, when thought comes in contact with the cosmic fires the records produce creation, and the spirit that attracts the fires is affirming a link with the Cosmic Magnet.

278. The centers of the Agni Yogi affirm all the cosmic fires. When an Agni Yogi hears a resounding, the link between the centers and the cosmic fires is manifested. This experience is the first achievement toward the establishing of a link with the far-off worlds. Therefore, the tension of the centers is very high and great caution must be manifested. It is a very important manifestation of saturation by Fire. Thus are We saturating the space. I so affirm!

279. All world upheavals and spiritual shiftings are governed by Fire. Only when Our Principle will be affirmed upon the planet will the era of Satya Yuga begin. All of human life proceeds aimlessly for those who do not accept the Perfect Heart and the sublimity of Reason. Only subtlety of assimilation will yield striving toward Fire. Verily, the centers of the Cosmos

are aflame with tension, and the spirit aspiring to the Infinite reverberates to these fires.

280. The striving of an Agni Yogi is in direct conformity with Cosmos. Thus, the centers of an Agni Yogi are in direct conformity with the saturated Fire of Cosmos. Man is accustomed to attach very little importance to his direct bond with Cosmos; he rejects the concept that each nerve, each vibration, manifests consonance with the cosmic tensions. The development of all feelings and of sensitiveness is possible through the centers.

281. The extent to which the conscious realization of cosmic attractions remains undeveloped is evident in human creativity. Toward what are efforts being directed? In what channel are all strivings gathered? By what impulse is humanity moved? Let us manifest understanding. Usually man dissipates his energy in an aimless striving to a vegetative life, excluding himself from the cosmic chain. Therefore, We say that a man can create his own world as a part of the World Community or become a link with the Cosmos and thus become a cosmic co-worker. Thus, striving brings one to Infinity.

282. This is why humanity is in need of those of Cosmic Consciousness. In the main, man's efforts are directed toward an existence devoid of consciousness. To know the future means to be affirmed in the present. To know the significance of Be-ness means to be convinced of the goal-fitness of existence. The cooperation with Cosmos is vividly expressed by the Carriers of Fire.

283. The basis of community is scientifically confirmed, and each principle expressed by a community will be activated by conformity with the World Community. The creativity of life may be developed upon

impetuous attraction toward the Magnet. Only a chain of aspirations to the expression of the worthiest principles will put humanity on the better step. Thus, beginning with the seed, the construction of a community can result in the Community of the World. One must reorganize all human undertakings in order that the consciousness may approach the Community of the World. Therefore, before the shifting there should not be fear but the affirmation of definite survival. Thus, through regeneration let us strive for the Community of the World. Only a broadened consciousness can give an invincible formula for community. When an affirmed step is being built, Cosmos acts through shifting. Verily, the hour will soon strike. Verily, the predestined will arrive.

284. Each striving is tensed by the lever of the heart. Only pure striving gives power to the spirit. This law is basic throughout Cosmos. Each element of Cosmic Fire is affirmed by the lever of the heart. The aura of aspiration of man is the most powerful moving force. The Lord manifests the fire of His Aura of aspiration. The Agni Yogi is intensifying the striving of an affirmed aura. Spirit-creativeness and the fiery centers of the Agni Yogi are creating a better step for humanity. How impetuous is the fire of the spirit of the Agni Yogi during the cosmic shiftings! Thus, when the striving toward the transformation tenses the planet, the power of cooperation invokes the Fire of Space.

285. Only when a substance is saturated with fire can it be said to be all-penetrating. Only when an action is permeated with fire does it create. Only when all torches are kindled does the Light smite darkness. Therefore, all which is constructed by Us withstands powerfully, and the basis of striving attracts the fiery impulses. We, Brothers of Humanity, create through

the lever of the heart, and We say, "The beauty of striving opens all paths."

286. When the rays intensify the impulsion of an energy, the striving cannot be arrested. When the spirit carries a magnet, as implanted within it, it is united with the Cosmic Magnet. When a new step is being built, the cosmic striving shifts all encumbrances. The law of shifting and the law of construction are directed toward the one focus. Therefore, all spatial shiftings are governed by the law of construction. The manifestation of the law of shifting tenses all spheres.

287. The cosmic sword is tensed by the awareness of a shifting. Only attraction pulls toward the Magnet. Those strivings which go against the current of the Cosmic Magnet alert a multitude of consciousnesses through the symbol of the sword. The developed spirit gives the power of consciousness to the sword, and the cosmic striving develops the impulse of urgency. Thus, the measure of spirit imparts to the consciousness the impulse of creativeness.

288. The sword of the spirit impels all tensed consciousnesses. Each consciousness which strives to a shifting creates in collaboration with the Cosmic Magnet. Thus, We create with the sword of the spirit. Therefore, Our co-workers create with the sword of the spirit. The creativeness of an Agni Yogi tenses the consciousnesses through Fire.

289. When the cosmic fires come in contact with the centers, the maximum tension occurs. Those who have adhered to the creativity of the centers gain a link with the Cosmic Magnet. Only when the centers are responsive to all cosmic attractions can the future be fierily defined. Thus, We strain the cosmic creativeness.

290. The creativeness of the centers is strained by the cosmic fires. When a cosmic shifting occurs the

fiery process can be manifested with especial vividness. When the fire of the spirit coalesces with the cosmic fires, it creates cosmically. Hence, Our flaming Mother of Agni Yoga must manifest Fire to humanity in the Epoch of Maitreya during the great period of shifting. Thus are We fulfilling a great ordainment.

291. Each new step of evolution requires a shifting. When the straining elements tense the Cosmic Magnet, the new steps are defined by Fire. Thus, the departing forces activate the new energies.

292. The tension of the centers is manifested as a consequence of the cosmic fires. Indeed, the centers sense all cosmic perturbations. An Agni Yogi senses all currents.

293. Cosmic thought is intensified by the impellent Cosmic Magnet. Spatial thought is strained by the lever of the Magnet. All human thoughts are impelled through harmonization with the Magnet. All forces which accompany the Magnet in all actions are intensified by the process of striving. Therefore, all oppositions to the impellent Magnet derive their strength from the realization of reverse currents. One can affirm the tension of energies through the concordance of all centers. Oppositions call forth tension in Cosmos, which aids creativeness Thus, all conscious energies create evolution.

294. Certainly all cosmic fires are sensed acutely by the Agni Yogi. All ailments of the Agni Yogi are of course of a cosmic character. Therefore, one must take care of the sensitive organism. It is a most important time, and the creativity of the centers is great! Thus, we reveal the centers to humanity. Each offering to humanity has its vast consequences.

295. People are afraid most of all of expansion of consciousness. Everything within the boundaries

of the customary is very close to man, and each new thought arouses opposition. Therefore, when We send someone for an achievement, We first impart the urge toward a new consciousness. Only limitless striving toward expansion of consciousness and reaching for the unusual can advance the consciousness toward evolution.

296. The expansion of consciousness is the goal of Our striving, and when Our co-workers carry this vessel a full cooperation is affirmed. Thus Our Brothers create, expanding the consciousnesses. The great experiment of Agni Yoga will bestow upon humanity the expansion of consciousness and the greater understanding of the two worlds.

297. Human constructions correspond very little with the foundations of Be-ness! The course of evolution can be affirmed by energies still unmanifested. But the fact that man has applied the revealed forces of Cosmos with such lack of commensurateness attests the retardation of evolution. The human understanding makes each formula given so inapplicable that its manifestation verily clogs the space with its issue. States, governments, families have become so distorted in human understanding! Thus, the expansion of consciousness will provide a new step of Infinity.

298. Every thought of an Agni Yogi is like a pearl for the regeneration of consciousness. Thus is the space imbued by Our Brothers. Certainly, a country propelled by a mechanical system cannot achieve much without the destruction of the old. Therefore, We value each creative thought, and the gold of the entire world will not buy the growth of thought.

299. The correlation of cosmic forces is so tense that the consciousness of humanity is striving toward saturation by Fire. In the construction of forms, each

force acquires the power of the existing fire, and each step of regeneration is suffused with a new understanding. Fire creates spiritually and intensifies all formulae. Thus, the consciousness progresses limitlessly.

300. The centers are strained into opening under the creativeness of the solar rays. In this stage of the experiment the solar plexus corresponds in rotation with the sun; therefore, each rotation of the solar plexus establishes a link with the Cosmic Magnet. This is one of the important confirmations of the experiment of Agni Yoga; therefore, it is most essential to protect the solar plexus from tension after sunset.

301. Humanity is so dreadfully afraid of the Unknown. As every sensation is established from an inner manifestation linked with the outer world, so does humanity confirm the various aspects it receives. How may one define the life of each being? In the material world every entity exists through ceaseless motion. Therefore, in place of the Unknown there may be substituted an eternal motion into Infinity.

302. For the physical eye, all manifestations are in the visible world; but the spirit-consciousness knows how moves the Universe. Therefore, the experiment of Agni Yoga and the spirit-creativeness link the visible and the invisible.

303. In each instance of human reception there is so much striving to blend with the cosmic energies that it is difficult to isolate a spatial manifestation. Besides the evident manifestations, humanity has had to create the measure of time, because without the creation of steps humanity cannot confirm itself in its growth. Thus, each measure of construction provides a step of evolution.

304. The ways of action differ in their tensions. The spirit striving to a cosmic action always displays the acceptance of cosmic measures. The ways of action of the spirit impelled to egoistic intensity always further measures that retard evolution. Thus, all the ways of action are strained by the human lever of intentions. Our planet is battling in a vigorously asserted tension, and the ways of action thus are turning the karmic effects. Therefore, the field of human ways clutters the sphere with dams.

305. In the ways of action are expressed all kinds of spiritual quests. He who strives, who has renounced, who is self-sacrificing, manifests his tension thereby; that spirit does understand the Common Good. He who persists in selfishness affirms his own methods of action. Thus, the entire human circle battles eternally.

306. The measure of service to humanity impels the spirit to means of striving. When the spirit knows the measure of tension in the name of Good, then he consciously directs his possibilities. The circle of the spirit surrounds the aura of man with powerful striving. But the sick aura and the aura surrounded by a tortuous line create corresponding saturations in space. Such auras react in a dual manner upon those around them. In identical auras they evoke an increase of negative potentiality. In contrasting auras they evoke a double striving: to smite darkness and to serve the Good. But these sick auras are nurtured by the emanations of the healthy auras. How important it is for a sick aura to be conscious of its armor! It is most important to realize this law. Evolution progresses through Light.

307. If there is neither transmutation nor continuity in the process of any being, then how can one explain the life of the Universe? The law of extension is one and the same in the entire Cosmos, and all principles adhere to the same law. Therefore, each vital energy must exist in continuity. These extensions exist

in all sorts of modifications, and every spirit who has attained a conscious striving to the law of continuity realizes complete duration and vastness.

308. A length of such extension is called a path of manifested Be-ness. Therefore, when striving strains the spirit the consciousness ardently encompasses all cosmic fires. Each tensed wave reflects upon the centers of an Agni Yogi. The play of the cosmic energies reflects powerfully on the centers. Therefore, one must guard most carefully the heart—a precise indicator. Thus, one must watch all sensations. One must notice everything, for everything is significant and everything has its conformities.

309. When the energies come in contact with the planet diversity is established. Human receptivity intensifies the organization of forms. Only human contact puts forms into the Cosmos. While the existence of beauty has been ordained by the Will of Cosmos, it is humanity that has to affirm the realization of its might. The spirit is the assimilator and the transmuter—thus man must think. Each wave of cosmic energies has its predestination.

310. These sacred waves are carried to the spirit who sensitively absorbs them. Creativeness of the spirit depends upon sensitiveness of receptivity. Receptivity is accessible only to the centers. There can be partial receptivity; then the spirit evinces the attainment of a specialty. Of course, there is in the creativeness the affirmed direction of an all-embracing synthesis plus a specialty. Thus is life constructed! Hence, each spatial cliché is differently assimilated. The centers of an Agni Yogi assimilate the essence of all energies. The result is vast. Every new science must establish its principles before proclaiming its knowledge to the world. There-

fore, I affirm that the fire of the centers of the Mother of Agni Yoga is a great achievement.

311. Verily, the process of human thinking creates correspondences with the cosmic treasures, and thus each thought generates an affirmed page. The centers of thinking depend on the evidence of receptivity. Human needs bespeak plainly the direction humanity has taken. The principle of correlation is directly established. Therefore, an identicalness demands the establishment of evident striving.

312. In Our deeds thought corresponds to action. The creativeness of the spirit affirms all directions. Verily, the striving of thought gives the impulse to all creative beginnings. Therefore, each thought of an Agni Yogi creates at a distance.

313. Intensity in the expansion of consciousness provides the foundation for all thoughts. But do the ignorant understand it thus? Do denying materialists understand it thus? Everything is contained in space, and each form lives through multifold modifications. Therefore, the expansion of consciousness must give man a remolded understanding of space. Thus, each thought carries along the progress of all spatial energies. The creativeness of spirit links its seed with the Cosmic Magnet. Thus, the spirit is a most powerful expression of the Cosmic Magnet. Striving toward Infinity will afford the understanding of Our creativeness.

314. The manifested ascent is immutably built in connection with the creativeness of the energies of Space. The new science of Agni Yoga gives the methods required for the sensitizing of the receptivity. Through this fiery science will Space be cognized and the formula of Fire known. Thus, the science of the future is being immutably constructed.

315. The undertakings of man show potentialities of all degrees and direct all strivings into a center of tensity. The manifold human undertakings are strained by various essences. In evolution, the battles for the treasures of Space are clearly defined. Thus, the advancement of the grades of energies is within the power of humanity, and the degree of retardation of evolution rests also in the hands of man. Verily, two categories intensify the world of action. The Carriers of Fire and the opponents of evolution both assert the evolutionary battle. Thus, the progress of humanity proceeds by way of the battle of evolution.

316. Our principle of Fire is so intense that creativeness is precipitated toward the Source of Fire; and the Mother of the World directs Her rays into Our spheres. Only Our approaches will grant evolution to the planet and will determine the construction. Therefore, the evolutionary battle will resolve in Our victory, and every stone brought by the enemy will provide a step for the victory. Thus, We truly utilize each obstacle. Verily, a great creativeness! The Tara of Fire will impart a new science to humanity.

317. Adherence to the Cosmic Magnet imparts intense striving to the spirit. Human creativity proceeds along the channel of striving. Existence demands a realization of the qualities of strivings. Thus, each possibility can manifest only through goal-fitness. With goal-fitness as a basis, man can formulate the reason of existence. Matter is affirmed in manifested form through the spirit of man; thus, cause and effect establish the reason of existence.

318. The formulation of the principle of goal-fitness is very instructive. If humanity in its striving would manifest greater cognizance of this, our planet could take a new step. Humanity lives on, continuing in this lack of goal-fitness, and the results engendered are so multiple that the human spheres are dark. The period of subterranean explosions is in correspondence with the supermundane accumulations. The countries which are shrouded in clouds of noncomprehension of the Cosmic Magnet will suffer—thus let us remember. Therefore, the solar plexus, being in direct connection with the Cosmic Magnet, exhibits manifold signs of perturbations. The knowledge of the Chalice very often brings anguish. Indeed, the planet is bathed in human tears. Thus, the Cosmos strains the centers of an Agni Yogi; the subtleness of the organism manifests a responding vibration. Thus do We serve Cosmos.

319. The consciousness and understanding of the world is tautened by the lever of spirit. Each spirit creates his own world, and the beauty or ugliness of the created world depends upon the quality of consciousness. Thus, only realization of cosmic energies gives creativeness to the spirit. But the spirit who denies the essence of the Cosmic Magnet is banished into the domain of ignorance. One may tell humanity that the world it has created does exist but that the world of true striving dwells in a fiery consciousness and in Infinity.

320. Worlds of the Infinite; worlds affirmed; worlds of harmony; worlds bounded; worlds of Light and of darkness—thus does humanity create and affirm the field of action. Thus is the creativeness of humanity manifested. Each thought which invades the space produces a form. These thoughts fill the worlds with their powerful vibrations. Thus, the fire of the spirit produces its own world. But the spirit bent on the frigidness of negation creates a world of darkness. These two factors produce the battle of Space. The flaming centers sense the entire battle; hence, each center responds to the spatial vibration.

321. Unmanifested matter is brought into life only through its spiritualization. Only form gives to matter the manifestation of life. But the spirit must be affirmed in the understanding that although matter receives the gift of the bliss of life because of its spiritualization, the process itself depends upon the potentiality of Eternal Fire. Thus, the thought formulates the action, but the potential of the spirit creates. Humanity is divided therefore according to the potential of the spirit.

322. Who, then, creates by the power of the spirit? The Bearer of Fire, the keen servitor of evolution, the creator of men, the one who gives all his fires for the growth of humanity. Humanity must be like these Light-Bearers in its quests.

How, then, does the Hierarch create on Earth? By uplifting all the surroundings. Thus, all spheres are uplifted by the pure flame of the Hierarch.

323. The stratifications of the planet constitute the foundations of the effects determined by Karma. By striving to the finest energies humanity will surround itself with a corresponding manifestation. Therefore, since the spiritual ascent is so slowly made by man, the declared step of stratification is executing pressure upon the earthly crust. The earthly fumes are quite intense and the earthly currents are very heavy. Therefore, there are very many perturbations in the earthly sphere. Thus the prophecies are being confirmed.

324. When We said that an Agni Yogi senses all tensions, We thereby alluded to the catastrophes. Each movement of the convulsion reacts against the centers like a wave. Each spatial battle tenses each center. Each arrow which comes from Our Towers alerts the centers. Therefore, the organism of Our Mother of Agni

Yoga is under great strain. Great is the spatial battle. Of course, Our nearness has a powerful impact, and the waves attest the fiery tension.

325. The earthly strata are greatly tensed because all earthly centers are atremble in the effort toward shifting. Every step of the cosmic shifting evokes tension. Thus, both matter and spirit are acting. The spirit immerging into the affirmed sphere of evolution is under the attraction of the Cosmic Magnet. How, then, can a spirit who does not carry the fires be affirmed? Each step of evolution is constructed by the Cosmic Magnet. Only when the spirit can build the step of cumulation of the Chalice can he become a co-worker of the Cosmic Magnet. Every effort to go beyond the limit of the usual pertains to constructiveness. Having stepped beyond the earthly strata, the spirit understands the needs of Earth. Thus, verily, will the spirit realize the Infinite.

326. The law of striving carries all affirmations. Striving toward Good avails itself of all higher paths, but wrath, which is in opposition to the Cosmic Magnet, adopts the basest ways. Hence, the dark forces in Cosmos are intensified by the lower spheres. At the moment of decisive shifting, the creativeness of nations is vividly expressed, and Cosmos strains the forces of Light for victory. Thus, the streams of Light conquer in limitless cosmic action.

327. The images of the spheres surrounding the nations represent the qualities of the stratifications. The spirit of a nation always preordains the substance of the future. The karma of effects vibrates around each nation; therefore, while the people strive so much after the foundations of Truth, only the elect advance by its channel. The conception of Truth is distorted above everything. Hence, when We say Truth, We call to the mastery of subtle energies and to the Cosmic Magnet. One can determine each national vibration. The truest indicator is the thought of a nation. The evidenced striving gives the key to cognizance of it. Thus, the national spirit builds the steps.

328. One can affirm that an Agni Yogi does not have purely physical pains. All the physical pains, which but demonstrate the presence of subtle energies, are called fiery; hence, each tension arouses sacred pains. The sensitiveness of assimilation is so powerful that one must chiefly avoid strain.

329. The world which is in contact with each spirit is an expression of his own striving. The spirit which senses its strained currents must strive to the course of the Cosmic Magnet. But is the creativeness of its spheres thus affirmed by humanity? Each spirit which strives to link itself to the Cosmic Magnet will find its own creations manifested. But the spirit bent on selfhood creates a doomed world. These worlds saturate the space and each one sets up a perturbation. In Cosmos everything is linked, and for this reason humanity bears the responsibility for each created sphere. Thus are the cosmic spheres created.

330. What a beautiful creative world the Agni Yogi builds around him! The spheres are verily suffused by a living fire of thought. When thought tenses the spheres, the spatial fires resound. These thoughts are like a piercing clang! The manifestation of thought sets up a vibration in the space. Therefore, Our creative impulse is a fiery thought.

331. When the world is in convulsion, how is it possible not to realize the cosmic shifting? When the world exists for evolution, how is it possible not to strive for true construction? In the great construction everything is predestined to be reworked, and the chief concern of humanity should be the quality of its contribution. Therefore, when We intensify all creative impulses, how then is it possible not to cognize the constructivity of Cosmos? The beauty of Be-ness is contained in the realization of all the subtle energies. In this principle is comprised the entire limitless creation.

332. When the world is atremble the subtle energies are being attracted to the planet. Therefore, humanity must realize that this is the hour of destruction and shifting and that a New Dawn glows upon the horizon. The creativity of Cosmos is incessant, and incessant is the replacement of some levers by others. When old conceptions of world evolution are becoming extinguished the dawn of the fires is kindled. Verily, the time is a fiery one, and Agni Yoga takes the place of all the departing energies. Thus do We kindle the New Dawn, and the waves of cosmic reconstruction are most powerful. All the centers vibrate, reverberating with the cosmic reconstruction. It is a great Dawn, and humanity can find in it the path to evolution. Thus, the light of Our fires will give humanity a new impulse. Yes, yes, yes! I so affirm!

333. So much has been affirmed by the Lords in regard to the future of humanity; yet the spirit ponders little upon the problems of affirmed existence, and the past prepares for humanity manifestations of difficulty. Creativeness depends upon the combination of energies. The future also is thus affirmed. Much has been told to man about the preordained creativeness and about predestination. This destiny man must realize. Our established law points to the impellent factor in the process and one should realize that the future is the result of the past. Thus, the striving of the spirit to a karmic consequence produces the predication of the future.

334. Those who have understood Our Teaching must approach most cautiously the determination of their own actions. The luminous future is being created under Our Shield. One cannot attain save through pure striving, but the fetters of selfhood encircle the Teaching with misconception. Therefore, it is very important to penetrate into the nature of the striving manifested. Verily, the many broad possibilities will bring a broad understanding. I so affirm.

335. The predetermination of the future is greatly intensified when there is affirmed a consequence of striving to the Cosmic Magnet. When this consequence comes into force, each of its steps achieves its own form. The chain of epochs is molded by the way of predestination. Thus, knowing the present, one can predetermine the future. One may determine every magnetic vibration that produces the striving of a nation. The study of causes will produce definite results. Thus, let each nation trace the fundamental quality of its aspirations and yearnings. The best indicator will be spiritual progress. Thus, through limitless striving there is established an intensive advancement into evolution.

336. Absence of coordination between energies forces explosions in Cosmos. Is there such lack of coordination between the energies of spirit and of thought? Each energy lives through its impulse. Each thought lives through its potentiality. Cosmic energy drives an intense striving into action. Human thought creates only through the lever of the heart. The word not imbued by the heart cannot create. Thus, without coordination between the word and the heart there is created only an explosion in space.

337. Indeed, We value sincerity above everything. The word which does not contain the affirmation of the heart is void. Only the potential of spirit can give power to creativeness. Thus, every thought bereft of this wondrous fire is deprived of life. Hence, each thought intensified by the heart is revered by Us.

338. In the realization of the coordination of energies there is contained the entire cosmic creativeness. That is why it is so imperative to strive to coordination. The entire cosmic power is comprised in this law. The application of the higher understanding of cosmic coordination will give direction to the spirit. When the spirit asserts its freedom, the direction depends upon the choice of paths. Thus, the coordination between the spirit and Cosmos is intensified by the potentiality of the seed. Lack of balance of the spirit is very destructive, because each one who approaches Us bears the karma of his attainments. Thus, the spirit-creativeness is directed by the spirit into a freely chosen cosmic stream.

339. Destiny is being fulfilled by the planet, and the cravings of humanity pierce the space. Therefore, in affirming the principles of Our Teaching many definite answers are accumulated for the development of humanity. By accepting the Teaching in the dead-letter sense the spirit does not ascend.

340. When an energy is shifted multifold forces are strained into action. During the shifting of a country all levers come into play. Creativeness, which leads to the Cosmic Magnet, is tensed by the lever of Light. But when a flux of the dark forces pulls toward destruction, all cosmic forces come into action. Visible tension brings into play only visible action. Invisible tension acts invisibly. Thus, each impellent striving

has its spheres of action, and the national shiftings are intensified through two channels.

341. Certainly, a country which has lost its direction cannot find the proper course of action. Certainly, a country which adopts the basest means is unaware of the higher manifestation. A sinking country vigorously fights for life. It is for this reason that We are under such strain; the mightiest current is created in the mightiest tension. Thus, We create, and the enemies sense Our nearness.

342. Permeation of the space by a manifestation of the spirit is conscious striving. When human thought penetrates beyond the boundaries of manifest Earth, this contribution is acknowledged in a gift to humanity from space. Every thought propelled into Space means loftier attainment. In the striving of thought is comprised a new achievement in spatial records. Each expanded thought carries the spirit to the summits of Space. Thus, the spirit who knows the flights beyond the limits of Earth can realize the creativeness of Infinity.

343. The spirit's bringing of various records from beyond the boundaries of Earth is that link which unites the spirit with the higher worlds. Each offering results in conscious striving of spirit. The Carrier of Fires directs humanity to the understanding of the creativeness of spirit. Thus, the experiment of the Mother of Agni Yoga gives a new impetus to humanity.

344. Adherence to the Cosmic Magnet can disclose to the spirit all paths to the General Good. Whither can the spirit strive that has not realized his direction? Wherewith can the spirit suffuse the mind? How can the spirit connect himself with the higher worlds? All cosmic forces can imbue the spirit with understanding of the path. Only Cosmic Might will indicate to a man

a conscious striving. When the spirit has cognized the course of the Cosmic Magnet, he can choose the path of his striving. Therefore, a sensitive receptivity guides the spirit immutably to the Cosmic Magnet.

345. We build new possibilities upon the sensitiveness of receptivity. The creative forces are especially powerful when they are strained by sensitive receptivity. Only when the strings of the sensitiveness of receptivity resound can one harken to the Cosmic Magnet; only then can the spirit gather all threads for creativity. The adherence to the Cosmic Magnet has impelled all Lords to the great self-sacrificing achievement. It is therefore that We value so much the heart which senses the course of the Cosmic Magnet.

346. When humanity lost all the sensitive threads of receptivity, fiery means had to be employed: the fiery sword of purification, the fiery sword of construction, the fiery sword of striving, the fiery sword of new energy. All the fiery tensions will give to humanity the creativeness of fiery saturation. Thus, the fiery sword brings to humanity when there is cooperation the ordained cosmic possibilities. And when the cosmic creativeness will be fierily affirmed all energies will approach. It is a decisive moment, and one which uplifts the human consciousness. Thus is human thought limitlessly saturated.

347. When there is cooperation with the cosmic forces the sensitive receptivity affords union with the manifestations of Cosmos. The Spatial Fire can impart creative tensity to the spirit which affirms its concordances. Therefore, since the spirit of an Agni Yogi senses all cosmic perturbations, the link with the Cosmos reveals to him all paths to knowledge. Thus, all cosmic forces resound upon the solar plexus. The

subtlety determines the quality of each reception. The whole of evolution is built upon this law.

348. Thought has definite significance as an affirmed impetus of creativeness. The diversity of Cosmos is intensified by the higher thought. Only when the aspiration toward thinking is realized can the subtle quality of energy be found. Since humanity speaks much about thought, certainly the significance of thought must assume a conscious form pertaining to the creativity of Cosmos. In the creativity of Cosmos each thought appears as motion. In human creativity thought is the impeller of each step, both in small and in great. The significance of thought is most powerful!

349. Pure thoughts carry one as wings; dark thoughts screen the horizon like flocks of black ravens. The spirit must realize this. The spirit must pronounce condemnation of its dark thoughts. Only a pure striving thought will affirm success. Therefore, each one who has adhered to the Teaching must be strengthened in the significance of thought. Verily, I declare that in the flight of the spirit the entire striving of thought is affirmed.

350. The broadening of consciousness is in the principle of the creative impulse. When Cosmos attracts the mind toward conscious cooperation, then a corresponding striving is affirmed. Therefore, the spirit that guards in its potentiality the creativeness which impels to conscious cooperation can intensify all fires. How important is the realization that each thought is applicable to life! Not by words but by thoughts is the world moved. Thus, each thought may help the cosmic energy.

351. Certainly creative thought will regenerate the world. He who masters thought creates evolution. Thus

We can move human consciousness toward progress. We create by thought.

Humanity, truly, must realize the significance of thought! The Teaching, truly, must be embraced by sensitive thoughts! Each striving thought can impel the spirit to achievement. Hence We value so highly the ability to shape one's thoughts. Each great thought is joined to the Chain of Hierarchy. Thus is evolution built.

352. Each sensing of the cosmic energies gives impetus to the communion with the Fire of Space. When the centers of earthly fires are active, tensions of the spatial fires are inevitable. When the Cosmos is strained, there are no inert energies. The volcanoes are becoming active and they evoke human tensions. Thus, when humanity has been brought into tension by the creative fires of shifting Our soaring flight is intensified by the Cosmic Magnet. Hence, the spirit who knows the dates and the course of the Cosmic Magnet can sense the volcanic actions upon the physical and spiritual planes.

353. The enemies are afraid of these volcanic actions. The volcanoes of the spirit are active, and the instinct of the enemies leads them to detect the Carriers of Fires. Only the Fire of Our Towers can conquer. The volcanoes are acting and the strongholds of the enemies are being destroyed.

354. The currents are strained in Cosmos for an upheaval. Each cosmic wave brings its energies. The spirit of the planet is strained in connection with the cosmic energies; thus, each cosmic stream tautens the strings of the spirit. In the shifting of the cosmic energies, the impulses of cosmic fires are strained. Thus, each string of spirit conforms to the stream of Cosmic Fire.

355. What power is contained in the formulation of a thought! One's whole creativeness goes into a formulation of thought. One may assert that the striving to a conscious formulation of thought already impregnates the thought with life. Only the knowledge resulting from pure striving gives creativeness to thought. Hence, all shaggy thinking results in corresponding formations. These defects of the spirit are so prickly, and the protecting net suffers so greatly from these projected needles! Our co-workers must learn to think without needles.

356. What might is contained in the creativeness of the heart! All cosmic tensions can be discharged by a light-bearing ray. How can one melt a projected arrow? Only by a smiting ray of Light. Therefore, the smiting ray of Light must penetrate into all arising difficulties. All the dark corners where ignorance is hiding must be illuminated. All erections based upon ignorance and cleavage should be demolished, because they do not further the growth of the construction. When We construct We manifest pure striving. All harmful accumulations of which humanity is unaware breed impediments to evolution. Thus, the smiting ray of Light will illumine all dark corners.

357. A manifested formulation of thought can create a chain of better effects. Only the manifestation of striving affords formulation of thought. How can one cognize the construction of the world? Only by the formulation of thought projected into the higher spheres. If humanity would but ponder upon adaptation of the higher structures, how easily it could apply the principle of expanded conception! Thus, adoption of the concept that all vital principles exist upon all planes will induce the formulation of thought.

358. Cosmic law calls humanity to the application

of the principles. The earthly laws are distorted by humanity. The higher laws are illumined by the spirit and the heart of the Arhat. Space is subject to these two divided conceptions. But the essence of cosmic existence proclaims that in Cosmos everything has its continuity, up to and into the beauty of Infinity.

359. A tensed psychic thought, in conjunction with the subtle feelings, gives the highest creative power. The creativeness of refined feelings is impelled by subtle energies. Only when thought is lawfully propelled into higher spheres do these strivings produce creative tensions. Therefore, the refinement of feelings and sensations is kindred to the tensed seeker of Fire. Cosmic thought can penetrate into a psychically refined consciousness. The realization of both subtle and crude assimilations will mark the first step in the progress of humanity. Thus, on the way to the Towers, one must remember the subtleness of psychic thought.

360. Subtlety of receptivity is necessary for an understanding of the Teacher. In the realization that the Teacher imbues the disciple's spirit with higher understanding is contained the entire progress of the disciple. The creativeness of the spirit can be impelled upward only when thought ascends. The link between the Teacher and disciple is forged by spiritual striving. Truly, who will uplift the spirit of the disciple if not his Teacher? Only the Higher can uplift the lower. Without this understanding it is impossible to advance. Thus, let us conclude by stressing the refinement of receptivity.

361. All psychically subtle organisms assimilate the cosmic currents. When thought contacts the higher spheres, it is imbued by the currents of Spatial Fire. Thus, when the earthly sphere is suffused with Our streams the fiery tension is affirmed. The sensations

of a psychically subtle organism differ greatly from the sensations of coarse organisms. Hence, only the refined receptivity can respond to the higher currents.

362. Verily, only through the refinement of receptivity can one sense Our wishes. Only the Agni Yogi in his subtleness can know all ways of attainment. Verily, everything is accessible to the higher Agni Yogi!

363. Subtle sensing by the centers foreordains a subtle creativity. All creative impulses under the strain of subtle sensations affirm subtlety in the forms. Therefore, humanity must affirm its striving to subtle sensations. All beautiful forms of Cosmos are built upon the subtlety of sensations. All refined feelings create refined forms. In Infinity, humanity can refine its sensations.

364. Cosmic sensitiveness fills the space. Only when an attraction acts upon a sensitive receptivity can a formula be affirmed. Therefore, when a cosmic combination is impelled to fusion, it is a power of sensitiveness that creates. Thus limitlessly does the Cosmos create sensitive organisms.

365. The sensitiveness of sensations unites all humanity in the higher spheres. This principle unites the Teacher with the disciple. Thus, sensitiveness is a chief quality of the disciple. Sensitiveness applied by the spirit gives keenness of perception. Thus, by applying the sensitiveness of the heart one may reach the highest aspirations.

366. When the energies affirm a new course, then the tension is great. Each striving attracts new possibilities. In a cosmic striving, the scale of affirmations manifested in Cosmos is disturbed; it is therefore that human actions are unsteady and countries are destroyed. Thus, the cosmic creativeness can maintain

the balance in a shifting. Great and full of power is the moment of shifting!

367. Verily, a great page! Verily, the Banner unfolds powerfully. Verily, when the world is in convulsion We intensify the forces of the higher means. But the front of opposition uses the lowest means. Therefore, the most powerful possibilities are being brought forth. Hence, Tactica Adversa is Our measure.

368. The entire power of the spirit is contained in the cosmic understanding. All the applied formulae must conform to the higher understanding. Only in cosmic understanding is contained the creativeness of the spirit. Only the commensuration of action with beauty gives the formula of life. Thus, the creation of better evolutionary steps can be asserted through commensuration with beauty. The spirit must aspire to this great principle.

369. When the creativeness of Cosmos is strained, all energies are directed into an intensive construction. Therefore, each directed power must be intensified in the search for new constructions. The creativity which reaches new correlations acts through the lever of Light. The Spatial Fire is putting all spheres under strain. The spirit of humanity is interlocked with Cosmos to such an extent that feelings are intensified by the same levers. Thus, in boundless creativeness one can imbue space with subtle strivings.

370. Thought penetrates into all spheres and fixes there its imprinted affirmations. There is creativeness in the fixing of new impressions upon the consciousness. Every energy has a creative power. The most subtle consciousness has the best receptivity. The most striving consciousness can affix the imprints of its thought. The creative power is affirmed by the centers possessing subtle receptivity. Each fine energy

is reflected in the creativeness of the spirit. Thought creates and it affirms each imprint! Thus do the Lords create. Likewise does an Agni Yogi create. If humanity would understand how majestic the creative impulse of thought is, then every thought generated would be expended for the Common Good. Thus, each pearl of spirit creates better possibilities.

371. The energy that destroys the tension of cosmic forces is the very subtle might that builds new possibilities. The creativity of energies is comprised in the shifting of old accumulations. Only when the power of destruction gives way to other powerful impulses can the cosmic shifting be asserted. The impelling creativeness of the Magnet can be defined as the spirit of the shifting. Only thus can one build the cosmic steps. The coming evolutionary movement proceeds by way of shifting. Thus, life is built by progression in the drive of cosmic magnetic power. Limitless is the cosmic creativeness!

372. Each intensified force has its affirmed opposition. Each intensified force has its purpose. The bridges consolidated by the enemy are the best ascent. Only when all adversaries are strained in opposition can the greatest plan be introduced into life. Thus, every foundation employs Tactica Adversa.

373. The harmonious plan of Cosmos is saturated by various currents. These currents seek contact with the spirit. Only a small quantity of the currents has been assimilated by humanity, and the main channel of vital actions is that of the currents set up by subtle assimilations. Only where there is conformity can the levers be tensed. Only where the Spatial Fire can reverberate to the subtle harmonies can a cosmic concordance be established. Therefore, a step of evolution is introduced into life through the subtle receptivity.

374. The Spatial Fire is assimilated by the centers of an Agni Yogi. Great is the laboratory when the subtle currents are assimilated. Who can transmit to humanity the subtle currents? Only an Agni Yogi through his high thought. If during the process of evolution instinct has developed into feeling, then refinement will lead to straight-knowledge. Each refined sensation means contact with the Spatial Fire. Therefore, only the highest Agni Yogi transmits to humanity the subtlest receptivity. The entire evolution is based on refinement.

375. The more attacks there are the more possibilities approach. In cosmic creativity, the balance is thus maintained for the development of new affirmations. The energy which develops a powerful stream strains all impulses. Only the power of cosmic shifting can bring new forces into tension. The power of shifting is so intense that the propelled forces encountered but saturate the striving. Thus, the harmonious order of cosmic creativeness is intensified by cosmic shifting.

376. Each thought given to humanity is for execution. Otherwise, why saturate the space? The lack of executors complicates the creation. Each thought given for saturation of the consciousnesses must find executors. The great spirit is a creator and each thought must enter into life. Vital action is the application of the thoughts of the great creators. Therefore, when humanity will be imbued by the realization of the application of thought, it will be possible to affirm that all the principles of higher dimensions have entered into life. Thus, the manifestation of shifting is commensurate with the application of thought in life. Only striving to a vital action produces shifting. Thus, the step of evolution is built by the thought of creators and its vital application.

377. Beautiful is the thought about Brotherhood upon Earth. Each disciplining of spirit produces striving. Only the will can give discipline to the spirit. But when the thought rambles, asserting selfhood, then verily there is no channel for true vital action. Every applied thought will bring growth to the spirit. Thus, each applied thought furthers the expansion of consciousness.

378. When a great structure is being built, each measure must be commensurate with it. When the outer image is imbued by fleeting efforts, then certainly the creative force is not lasting. But when each measure glows with the inner fire the structure can endure. Therefore, when the power of the spirit illumines the construction, success can be affirmed. In Cosmos, a vital action is intensified by the impulse of the inner fire. Every energy is moved by this potentiality. Every vital measure is moved by the fiery spirit. The realization of this principle can advance the trend of thought; therefore, when striving produces creative tension the subtle energies will be attracted.

379. Indeed, above all We value constructions based upon the higher principles of harmony. Of course, each subtly assimilated thought will be as the foundation for a sensitive action. The creativeness of beauty is built upon this principle, and the power of harmony is thus affirmed. Only in unity can mighty structures be created.

380. When a great structure is built, each page has its significance. Each affirmation of the cosmic evolution is impregnated in conformity. It is correct to say that humanity builds its cosmic steps in its strivings and assimilations. Humanity either receives or gives out the manifested forces. Precisely, its Service to the Cosmic Good gives humanity its ascent. When the transport of human aspiration is limitless and endless, a cosmic coordination can be affirmed. How wondrous is the realization of the link with Cosmos! How beautiful is the building of cosmic evolution!

381. When the spirit understands that Service to Cosmos means bringing into life the higher principles, it strains its best levers. An aimless existence is the result of the slumber of all the higher centers. When the thought of a great spirit awakens the consciousness toward a higher understanding of Service, it can be affirmed that cosmic striving is being conferred upon humanity. Therefore, it is most important that the thought of Service should permeate humanity. The carriers of the higher thoughts of evolution affirm Our Will. Thus is being established the higher cosmic cooperation. Thus, We carry the Cosmic Service together.

382. The concept of humanity regarding the Universal Being differs so greatly from the Universal Essence that all definitions should be revised. When the meaning of Be-ness is permeated with the understanding of Omnipresence and Omnisuffusion, then verily the Cosmos assumes a Fiery Image. But if each energy is isolated in human understanding, then certainly the assertion of life proceeds in conformity. Upon the principle of correspondence depends the entire human existence. Thus, the degree of consciousness determines the quality of the evolutionary step, because the spirit itself and its striving are the foundations of existence.

383. The degree of consciousness is intensified according to the quality of the fires. When the consciousness is capable of subtle assimilation each fiery energy can be consciously sensed. Hence, the striving thought of an Agni Yogi is always in contact with the fiery current. Every thought of an Agni Yogi carries a

fiery striving and imprints a spatial record. Therefore, the creativeness of thought gives powerful impetus to evolution.

384. The cosmic tension is expressed in the driving force of all energies upon all planes. Therefore, the separation of the physical and spiritual worlds cannot lead to the understanding of the higher coordinations. Only when the principle of coordination is affirmed in the consciousness can one strive to assimilate the higher energies. The principle of coordination puts man into contact with the manifestations of cosmic fires. The principle of coordination impels the spirit to higher cognizance. Hence, the cognizance of the universal energy gives the spirit a knowledge of his own substance. When the spirit absorbs the higher impulses, it can be said that he creates with Cosmos.

385. Who, then, brings these higher energies to humanity? The subtlety and striving carry in themselves the affirmation of cosmic coordinations. These Fire Carriers impart to humanity subtlety and knowledge. All the forms are being created by the tensed carrier of thought. When the fires are saturating the space the shield of the spirit sends forth the fire of creativeness. Thus is each epoch created. Thus will the epoch of Agni Yoga enter into life.

386. In the reconstruction of the world each energy is assimilated by the cosmic current. Only when a human thought is taken hold of by a certain affirmed current can the cosmic effect be defined. Thus, each human striving is saturated by a human current, and each creative energy is attracted by the Cosmic Magnet. Therefore, conscious power saturates human striving. Thus, humanity carries out its designations into Infinity.

387. Humanity's conception of the world is quite

far from the truth. Only when the conception will correspond to Cosmic Truth can a proper striving be expected. The limitation of consciousness is the doom of the spirit; in it is contained a complete extermination of the best possibilities. Therefore, when the consciousness is limited by the visible world alone there is no link with Cosmos. Only that consciousness which embraces the world in the scope of vast actions can become a true co-worker of Cosmos. The law of cause and effect is so powerful that humanity must apply the understanding of the principle of coordination. It is customary to consider that time guides humanity, but this conception must be broadened. We say that the impellent force of actions in time moves each cosmic effect. Thus is Infinity created!

388. The filling of the space with the records of higher strivings is the highest stimulus of creativeness. Nothing can so strain and shift consciousness as powerful thought! The construction of basic principles is caused by and depends on the stimulus of thought. You have said correctly that each respecter of thought defined his epoch according to the quality of his consciousness. An epoch can be defined according to the stimulus of its thought. By this the new generation can be directed. The ability to discriminate in the stimulus of thought and its consequence can bring expansion of consciousness.

389. When the motion of cosmic tensions attracts the propelled forces into their orbits nothing can remove them from these currents. The vortex rings can both pull in and cast out. Thus, only a ceaselessly driven current can build the cosmic creativity. Only an identical power can draw in that which is identical. Therefore, when creativeness draws energies into its orbit, the vortices propel their properties accord-

ingly. In the shifting of spiritual tensions the same process takes place. Therefore, each energy can attract a mighty afflux of creativeness.

390. The spiritual tensions are subject to the law of identity. The vortices take hold of all spiritual strivings. Hence, when the spirit is strained toward a shifting, nothing can stop it. The creators of whirls saturate the entire space and pull cosmic thoughts into their orbits. Hence, each thought of an Agni Yogi is a vortex; and the flame of the spirit is intensified by the striving Agni Yogi. Thus, each striving thought creates a new orbit, and all tensions are so sensed by the centers of a flaming spirit.

391. The Cosmic Consciousness is reflected in all world structures. Only humanity is limited by inability to admit the integrity of existence. All points touch each other in Cosmos. A cycle of life lives in the limitless Cycle of Cosmos. The cosmic ray is diffused throughout Space. Only the human ray limits its spheres. Instead of reflecting in its spirit the entire manifested Be-ness, humanity steeps itself in the conception of a limited world. There is not division in Cosmos and the chain of events is closely linked throughout all planes. Hence, the cosmic perturbations and spiritual shiftings proceed in parallel. Thus, there is cycle within cycle; and in these limitless shifting planes the human karma flows toward the affirmation of Infinity.

392. The universal consciousness perceives the chain of spheres and the threads of the bond with the spatial energies. One cannot divide the affirmed spheres; the Great Universal Present blends all manifestations. Thus, the present awakening of Cosmos brings an awakening to the spirit. Events upon one plane stimulate events on a corresponding one and they also bestir the consciousness with the same might

as the cosmic tension of spatial fires. Therefore, the unity in Cosmos and the world conditions at present strain all lives. Hence, both the thought of the Cosmic Reason and that of humanity must be asserted in the cosmic course. A limitless cooperation!

393. Correct is the term *cosmic dross*! Cosmic striving encompasses all cosmic manifestations but the spirit limited by the idea of isolation cannot create in step with the pulse of Cosmos. Hence, when a step of evolution is being built cosmic dross acts like dams. Certainly, each dam creates a heavy karma. Therefore, We distinguish the manifested Carriers of Light from the cosmic dross. The fire of spirit brings to humanity the striving toward higher principles.

394. Consciousness and thought create cosmic steps. What is then the attitude of humanity toward universal energy? It conceives this cosmic energy from an angle opposite to the correct one. If the spirit does not acknowledge the Fire suffusing everything, how then can it accept the cosmic energy? And chiefly, how can it affirm within itself the spark of creativeness? Verily, the spirit affirms its potentialities through realization that consciousness and thought create.

395. When a thought saturates the space, its power is in conformity with Cosmos. Every rational energy reflects upon the thought. Verily, thought and consciousness bring forth all cosmic principles and creativeness. Hence, humanity must broaden its understanding and strive to the realization that each energy can receive life and form only through the impulse of thought. Thought is the mover of evolution. Each one who has dedicated himself to Service saturates everything with his fire. When a thought is straining forth with an inner fire, the centers are aflame.

396. The striving will creates multifold combinations. Only when thought leads to the realization of desire can one create. Everything is contained in striving. The foundation of every action is striving. Hence, the more vividly the striving is expressed and the more clearly the realization is formulated, the more powerfully does the striving create. Men do not know how to wish. Men do not know the measures leading to creativity. Men do not direct their desires toward achievement. Whereas, each aspiring thought can liberate the spirit from cosmic dross. Thus, thought will assist the desire and the psychic energy. How greatly psychic energy moves life! The formulation of the desire gives impulse to creative manifestations. Thus, the thought intensifies each creative energy.

397. He who is desirous of realizing the creative Magnet must understand the power of striving. He who has accepted the Chalice of Amrita knows the striving thought. Only when a powerful assimilation can be affirmed is the tension in step with that of the Magnet. Verily, the centers then resound with the Cosmic Magnet. The Carrier of Fires imparts to his desires a tense striving. Hence, each fiery thought conforms to the tensed Magnet. Therefore, the thought of the Carrier of Fires is in itself of cosmic creativeness, and wishes of the Carrier of Fires powerfully advance evolution.

398. Of all energies, thought is the subtlest. It can be truly asserted that thought outlives everything. Thought is immortal; it lives on by creating new combinations. Hence, when the power of psychic energy is intensified, nothing can block it. When the consciousness of a people demands new steps, the power of psychic energy must be asserted and then propelled into space. The realization that thought is eternal and invincible will evoke in humanity the striving for the generating of creative thought. When the thought saturates the space, its impelling magnetism creates. Limitlessly is the space thus cemented!

399. Thought comes in contact with the Spatial Fire in, as it were, a mutual saturation. Therefore, when thought enters life, cosmic force creates. Hence, those who bestow on the world creativeness of thought give life to humanity. We affirm that the gold of the entire world cannot buy a creative thought. Verily, Our co-workers must expand the consciousness.

400. In essence, each action in the world has a meaning. In essence, every object has a meaning. But if the thought which colors the objects and actions springs from nullity it does not touch the cosmic current. Upon the essence of each manifestation life is built. Therefore, when Service calls for the creation of evolution, then there exists only the principle of Essence. Little do people know about discriminating in the Essence; little does the coloring by humanity correspond to the principle of Essence. Is every human thought affirmed in goal-fitness? Cosmic creativity is built upon the orbits of Essence. Thus, the ever-living is saturated by the subtle fires of the Essence.

401. Verily, when the essential constructiveness is impelled through the higher fires to give to the world a new step, there are no earthly standards for measuring it. Only that which has identity can produce the identical. That which is affirmed by the highest can be measured only by the highest, and all earthly colorings cannot measure Essence.

402. The consciousness embracing the measure of life can approach cosmic cooperation by affirmation of the existing. But when the application of vital principles impels the spirit to the law of higher dimensions the meaning of Be-ness is colored by the striving spirit. Thus, the Universe is cognized by each spirit individually, but the essence is cognized by him who has adopted a higher measurement. Every striving thought leads toward higher dimensions.

403. Each striving thought directed to cognizance of the Universe leads humanity into the higher dimension. Hence, each thought saturated by the fire of a striving Agni Yogi leads to the affirmation of evolution. Therefore, as the purpose of Existence points to the expansion of consciousness, each substance in the Universe points to the law of cooperation. Thus, each fiery thought leads to the affirmation of Essence in Cosmos.

404. The essence of construction is contained in consciousness. Only when the meaning of cosmic construction is understood can one apply the highest dimensions. Therefore, when the consciousness does not encompass the essence of cosmic construction it constitutes only a partial cognition. But a partial consciousness can grasp only a partial construction. Every integrated striving to cosmic construction is therefore most important, for in it there is evolution and evolutionary creativity.

405. When a Carrier of Fires participates in cosmic construction he brings a higher creativeness. Creativeness upon Earth is asserted by these Carriers of Fires, and only he who has embraced the cognition of higher dimensions can bring to humanity a saturated conscious magnet.

The Mother of Agni Yoga, having cognized the higher dimensions and the fiery creation, verily brings the essence of life. We, Brothers of Humanity, live and measure by the higher dimension.

406. The creativeness that molds the cosmic construction adheres to the Cosmic Magnet. Only when the higher dimension is totally applied can one attain cosmic constructiveness. Only when beauty is totally applied is cosmic constructiveness revealed. Those who have adhered to cosmic constructiveness can direct humanity to beauty. Only the application of the higher dimension can open the gates. Only the application of higher discernment will provide the key to cosmic creativeness. Thus, humanity must strive to the cognition of the higher dimension.

407. Construction awaits. Construction summons. Humanity must be affirmed in the understanding of this great call. The one who is a responsible recipient of Fire is a mover of humanity toward evolution. Hence, the subtle thinker is a mover of evolution. Thus is the cosmic striving being built. Thus thought moves humanity.

408. The energies being attracted are drawn toward a center of sensitivity. The striving of the spirit attracts the subtle energies and gives them life. Hence, the centers of an Agni Yogi inspire life. Thus We build a better step.

409. The creativeness of the spirit is so powerful that the solar serpent, having assimilated the affirmed cosmic fires, is manifesting concordance; therefore, the centers of an Agni Yogi vibrate fierily. All cosmic forces have become strained and the power of assimilation is growing.

410. Our creativeness surpasses the consciousness of men. Every constructive possibility is tensed by the Higher Powers, and We cooperate with the Higher Powers. Hence, the Cosmic Magnet affirms Our strength. Therefore, each wave of intensity promotes striving activity. Thus do We conquer; thus each wave coming forth from the heart must conquer.

411. Humanity gives much attention to the manifestation of the visible, whereas, every transitory energy is not a main impeller. How imperceptible to a limited sight are the main impellers! Only when the benevolent creativeness of Cosmos can be applied to construction will the striving for knowledge open the gates, disclosing the possibility of cooperation with Cosmos. Hence, each invisible might must be sensed by the spirit. Verily, thus are the steps of evolution built.

412. The highest spheres are invisibly linked. The most powerful strivings are invisibly linked. An invisible vibration links the spirits most powerfully. Thus, each wave of striving seizes upon identical energies. Hence, when an expanded consciousness sends out a powerful striving an identical striving toward creativity is exerted.

413. In the tension of cosmic fires is contained the entire creativeness of the subtle energies. Only the process of surging energies can create and expand all cosmic manifestations. How then is it possible for humanity not to accept the manifestations of the subtle energies! All spheres are interlinked and the cosmic bond is fused with the creativeness of the mighty Fire. The subtle energies are propelled into the spheres akin to them and each spirit chooses its own orbit. Thus, it is the same Fire that calls forth striving in each manifestation of the spirit.

A most sacred fire abides within the spirit of a true Agni Yogi. An impelling, immutable, invincible fire lies in the Chalice of Him who brings the Fire to humanity. Thus, limitless are the orbits of the expansion of consciousness.

414. Yes, only those subtle energies which contact the spirit can give creativeness to humanity. Only the beauty of the spirit can move humanity. The power of creativeness is contained in the fire of the spirit. Thus, the mighty Agni Yogi who breathes in the fiery impel-

lent force of cosmic fires gives to the world much of his heart and the flow of rays. The creativeness of the spirit expands in a radiant orbit. Therefore, when the spirit manifests a subtle assimilation of fires he then gives out the same amount to the world, preserving the equilibrium of creativeness. Hence, there is cosmic creativeness in each fiery assimilation. Thus is the cosmic evolution built. It is therefore that the qualities of the fire of the Mother of Agni Yoga are so sacred. It is thus that We build Our immutable actions. Thus is the future step constructed.

415. Only a vital interchange can produce a creative wave. Only the grandeur of Cosmos affirms the manifestation of a vital interchange. A cosmic seed is inlaid in everything and the Cosmic Fire is expressed in all. How then can humanity affirm its existence without the principle manifested by the vital interchange? The law of existence draws the spirit into the orbit of the cosmic seed, and when the spirit strives toward communion with the higher spheres, then the cooperation can be affirmed. Only when the interchange is imbued with a conscious striving can cosmic cooperation be affirmed. Therefore, each higher energy that is assimilated by the spirit can bring conscious striving to humanity. Thus, the manifestation of interchange provides a limitless cooperation.

416. The eternal interchange cosmically unites and impels toward consummation the particles which belong to each other. The creative power of Cosmos attracts the impelled particles of life which are driving toward the affirmation of consummation. Only when the spirit knows the manifested law can Cosmos powerfully attract. Therefore, when the thought of consummation summons, the particles speed toward fusion in fiery striving.

417. The grandeur of cosmos creates with the mightiest levers. The vital action is so much affirmed by the subtle energies that only the fires of Space can saturate this process. Thus, the striving of the seed and the intensity of the Spatial Fire create in an eternal interchange. Therefore, when cosmic power creates, an interchange takes place which arises from the inner impulses toward the cosmic seed. Every human action is saturated by the same attractions; hence, the spirit must strive so solicitously to those principles which will lead the striving one toward the cognition of the higher energies.

418. Each spirit must strive to the realization of higher attractions. The plans of the Lords give to humanity the cognition of the higher attractions. Who, then, imparts to humanity the higher cognitions? Only the Carriers of Fires. The higher attraction comes to the one who sensitively responds to all cosmic fires. Thus, the magnet of the heart is as powerful as the Cosmic Fire. The power of the spirit builds existence. The vital attraction builds the Cosmos.

419. The law governing the function of saturation is applied through attraction and identity of energies. When the impelled creative impulse gathers the affirmed energies in space, the law of the function of correspondence gathers the manifested fires. Humanity must understand that each force that enters into life creates upon the visible plane but is intensified by an invisible lever. Hence, one must seek in space for the saturating Fire and accept the law which serves as a link between striving and the creativeness of Fire. Thus, We strain the spatial manifestations into conformity with cosmic manifestations. The laws of spatial fires and human actions have identical driving force. Thus, the lowest attracts the lowest and the highest attracts the highest. But the law demands striving, and evolution is built by the manifestation of the higher attraction.

420. When the attraction of fires is intensified, all cosmic energies reverberate. Therefore, each principle acts through an impelling magnetism. Cosmic Fire itself is diffused through all that exists. Therefore, each cosmic wave strains the human consciousness. In this law is contained the entire power of creation. All earthly and cosmic fires can respond to the same law. Never has it happened that a human spirit has remained untouched by a cosmic wave. But only a spirit striving toward evolution can cognize the whole unity of Cosmos. Therefore, these cognizant spirits are the chief impellers of cosmic creativity. Thus, the key of knowledge creates a better step. Thus, Our Carriers of Fire affirm a better epoch. Thus, the invisible attracts the visible into the higher sphere. Thus, We fill life with the new quests. Thus, We create the manifestation of evolution.

421. Each manifestation of the invisible must be accepted by humanity as that of a principle leading to creativeness. In the entire Cosmos the manifestations of the invisible alternate with the visible. Therefore, when the space is saturated by a live interchange of Fire, a demarcation line does not exist. If the spheres were separated, transmission of cosmic power would be impossible. The vital threads cannot be separated. The All-Existent is in all and we are in it. Limitless is the vital potentiality, and the particles assimilated by humanity can conform to a cosmic striving only when consciously assimilated. Thus, in the cognizance of Cosmos one can strive to evolution.

422. Who, then, knows the requirements of evolution? Who, then, will gather the vital threads? Only the spirit understands how the invisible is interwoven with the visible. Only an expanded consciousness can understand how spirit and action are interwoven. Only a striving consciousness can impart to humanity the understanding of the higher energies. Hence, each thought conducive to the saturation of space brings to humanity the cognition of Cosmos. Therefore, when the thought of a Carrier of Fires saturates the space, it intertwines with the higher energies. Our vital threads are the interweavement of all consciousnesses and vital currents. The great past and the great future are interwoven in a radiant change of lives. Thus, Our orbit gives to humanity a new step.

423. When the shifting takes the visible form of manifested perturbations, the tensity of the cosmic fires brings all forces into action. Only when the thought attracts the Fire of Space does a discharge occur through the Cosmic Magnet. The magnetic waves aggregate all conscious energies. Humanity does not wish to realize the unity of the entire Cosmos. Cosmic creativeness fierily propels all elements, manifesting the one law; therefore, each wave strained forth by a people is but a link in the cosmic chain of evolution. Hence, when striving tautens the national wave, a shifting is then asserted. Thus, thought confirms the shifting, and the law of interchange motivates all impulses. The thinking of humanity thus produces the saturation of Space.

424. When Space thunders with the shifting, one must protect well those centers which respond. When the creativeness of Cosmos gathers the higher tensions, one must battle for the affirmation of Light. There is mutual intensification between humanity and the beauty of Cosmos, and only thus can one affirm a cosmically united power. Such striving has construc-

tiveness in it. The creativeness of thought has continuous inner blending, and the spirit of a cosmic creator knows the thought of Cosmic Reason. Thus, a sensitive Agni Yogi knows the flow of evolution, and each spatial thought finds corroboration. Each thought manifested by the fire of a creator imbues consciousnesses. Thus, We create the shifting of the spirit and affirm an enlightened cognizance.

425. The attainment of great cosmic steps can be assured through a conscious cooperation with cosmic energies. Conscious interchange can impart a full understanding of all the higher energies. Each striving to the orbit of the Cosmic Magnet will afford an achievement of a higher step. Thus, the law of great conformity is immutable. In building the cosmic evolution one must remember interchange. The space and the human spirit are saturated with these energies. It takes millennia to accumulate the impellent forces which proceed in a tense rhythm. The creative spirit knows these true impulses; and each will that conveys to the Cosmic Magnet the interchange manifested in striving gives to humanity the law of real correspondences. Therefore, it is so important to apply striving. The interchange impregnates all creative impulses.

426. Every striving in awareness of the future leads to creativity. So many beginnings array themselves upon the face of the Earth. How many unprecedented perturbations are being experienced by our planet! Only the spirit knows how to be affirmed in the orbit of the Cosmic Magnet, and it is thus that the fiery impulse in an Agni Yogi is asserted. The tension of the centers then is in direct ratio to the basic attraction. Thus are the centers drawn into the orbit of the Cosmic Magnet; and the attraction and harmony bring everlasting solemnity. Thus is Our creative drive affirmed. Of course, only spiritual attraction can intensify concordances. Therefore, the spiritual bonds are most strongly interwoven in the great march of the Cosmos. Thus do We construct Our steps.

427. The conditions of new scientific achievements must correspond to the demands of the future. If scientists would understand that the manifestation of continuous expansion underlies the growth of science, there would be no place for criminal antagonism. But We do not wish to upset their achievements—only to broaden them. Each scientist who understands the law of the expansion of consciousness has already smashed the wall of prejudice.

428. Knowledge, knowledge, knowledge! If people would ponder upon the fact that knowledge is the only salvation, there would not be a particle of the present suffering. All human sorrow is the result of ignorance. Therefore, every expansion of consciousness is cooperation with evolution. Every manifestation that obstructs the expansion of consciousness is antagonistic to evolution. Hence, the actions of the enemies are criminal and their karma is dreadful. Knowledge, let us reiterate, will put an end to the suffering of mankind.

429. Again one has to remind the scientists that the theories of Einstein do not upset the laws of Euclid but encompass them. Just as the third dimension does not nullify the laws of the plane, but is infinitely larger than the latter, so also the laws of spiritual knowledge encompass all your laws, being infinitely broader. Therefore, lay antagonism aside as an impediment to evolution.

430. A manifestation of magnetic storms underlies all the atmospheric perturbations. But the intervals between such manifestations are irregular and sometimes very extensive; hence, it is difficult to discover the law.

431. The distribution of currents issuing from the centers of magnetic accumulations produces the atmospheric manifestations. The law of interaction of the currents is in general the same as that of the electro-magnetic manifestations. But research and observations are needed, which will enrich humanity with a great discovery.

432. The magnetic currents affect greater areas than do electric manifestations. True, contemporary apparati are but playthings. Yet this domain of science is more accessible than the mystery of atomic energy. The force of action of even a small magnet is very great, but people are even unaware of its ways of direction and take cognizance of only its physical attraction.

433. Forces acting in direct opposition to each other are mutually annihilative. Forces acting in parallel and in the same direction are effective in their sum total and forces acting in opposition are decreased in proportion to the angle of divergence. Why cannot people acknowledge that this fundamental law of physics is also a fundamental law of cooperation!

434. The passing of magnetic currents over the earthly surface draws the lines of atmospheric changes. The passing of magnetic currents beneath the earthly surface brings into manifestation the earthquake belt. Certainly, observation posts should be established in many places, and their work should be most precise and closely coordinated. You spoke correctly in saying that it is unfortunate that there is no synthesis of achievements and thus much energy and many valuable observations are lost. Hence, the organization of real cooperation upon Earth is very essential.

435. The affirmation of cosmic attractions is

accepted by humanity in connection with great manifestations. Each attracted energy draws along with it a corresponding circle. Only an impenetrable mind cannot accept the property of correspondence. The attraction of cosmic forces gives to the planet all the powerful impulses; therefore, the construction of one's own orbit depends upon striving. Thus, each orbit which concludes the life paths is the creation of the properties of attraction. Thus one can advance into evolution on a limitless path.

436. The service to the Lords enters into the orbit of cosmic constructions. Thus, spiritual strivings enter into the orbit of cosmic attractions. All strivings of the spirit create like an affirmed fire. Thus, in Cosmos one can observe the manifestations of ceaseless creativity. Only the spirit who perceives the future can offer to Cosmos a striving in the name of true construction. Therefore, We create in the name of General Good. Yes, yes, yes!

437. How can one sense a cosmic shifting? How can one sense the Cosmic Might? All sensitive impulses must be drawn to the cosmic seed through striving and must direct the spirit to the understanding of vital energies. The affirmed strivings do not come from without; not accidentally is the spirit attracted to construction. The cosmic affirmation of the vital energies inherent in Fire exists in the entire manifested Cosmos. Thus, the construction of vital orbits depends upon striving. This fiery impulse lives in Infinity.

438. Who, then, will bring to humanity this vital impulse? Who will impart the understanding of the subtle energies? Only the spirit who is in possession of the vital impulse. One should not seek it in the asserted physical impulse but in the impellent invisible Fire which is the breath of life. Thus, the sensitive fiery spirit of the Agni Yogi brings to humanity the manifestation of the vital impulse. That is why the sensitiveness of these fiery impulses is so greatly reverenced by Us. Thus, it is the vital impulse that brings consummation—that vital impulse which is possessed by the Cosmic Reason and which saturates the Cosmic Consciousness. Thus, we all live by this fiery principle.

439. The pull of the fiery threads can saturate all spheres. The correlation between the spheres gives to Cosmos an impellent force manifested by Fire. Only the pull of cosmic threads can assert the properties of the spatial fires. Each sphere is consolidated by its properties. Thus, spiritual progress is permeated with the quality of conscious striving. Every fiery striving has its source in the properties of attraction. Therefore, when the cosmic shifting is determined the spiritual levers come into action. How, then, can a spirit be drawn to the seed of Spatial Fire? Only through the stimulus of correlation. Hence, the development of the cosmic fires induces striving. Thus, a surging fiery transport carries the spirit toward victory.

440. Certainly the spirit which stands close to construction can feel the correspondence between the planes. Hence, the correspondence attracts conscious impulsions. The creativeness of the spirit of a sensitive Agni Yogi knows the direction of magnetic currents. Hence, when all forces are intensified, human thought strains the levers of shifting. Therefore, the enemies feel all the mighty coordinations and the dark forces bar themselves from Light.

441. The cosmic shifting attracts all spatial fires, and the human spirit forms its own tensions. Only when humanity is attracted to new construction is it keeping pace with the Cosmic Magnet. Therefore, only the search for the ways of the Cosmic Mag-

net will bring to humanity the cognizance of higher energies. Thus, when humanity fills the space with its quests space responds by sending the higher energies. The attracted energy can take form in a vital application. Each thought induces concordance; upon this is life constructed. Therefore, only a conscious striving will take shape, and each possibility is affirmed by the attraction of thought. Thus, limitless are the ways of thought.

442. The thoughts of a fiery Agni Yogi are most powerful. The fiery energies are absorbed by him out of space and directed into a vital orbit. Therefore, when the thought of a fiery Agni Yogi strives to creativity, all the energies acquire vitality. Thus can each possibility be asserted in life. Obstacles call forth the surging thought, and the growth of obstacles is the best indicator of the greatness of the task. Hence, a fiery Agni Yogi is persecuted for his thought.

443. The quality of the energy intensifies each action. The power of the energy is not in the action but in the impulse. When a form is being created it is the quality of the energies that predetermines its vitality. Therefore, the creativity of the Cosmic Magnet should be defined as the manifestation of quality. Only creative energies send the impulsions toward the formation of vital fires. Therefore, when the thought cognizes every quality of striving, the Cosmic Consciousness can be affirmed. Hence, let us accept each manifestation of such quality as a move producing life. The creativeness of Infinity is saturated by the qualities of the energies.

444. The growth of consciousness consists in the discrimination in the qualities of the energies. Only through this knowledge can the spirit determine the cosmic creativeness. Hence, the knowledge of

the spirit leads to the discrimination in the qualities of energies. Thus, the subtle centers of an Agni Yogi know the ordainment of the Cosmic Magnet. Therefore, the enemy fears greatly Our knowledge. Hence such opposition and hence so many obstacles and so many great victories. Thus, We saturate the space.

445. The quality of the energy predetermines each human undertaking. The creativeness of the spirit is imbued by the quality of the energy. Human striving must be directed to the understanding of the quality of energy. The spirit will approach closely the knowledge of higher energies if it will cognize the entire saturation through Fire. In each impulse this fiery quality exists. Each vital striving is impelled by this quality. The realization of this quality will induce an understanding of all the vital impulsions of Infinity.

446. The creative impulse is imbued by a fiery quality. Therefore, all the fiery manifestations of an Agni Yogi direct in turn vital impulses. The impulsion of the vital Fire produces a chain of creative possibilities. Thus, the fire of the spirit imbues all vital strivings. The manifestation of unity permeates all Cosmos, and the entire diversity of vital manifestations is contained in the quality of Fire. Hence, the sensations of the Agni Yogi are so diverse. Therefore, the Mother of Agni Yoga can so reverberate to all cosmic perturbations.

447. The quality of thought impregnates the space, and each action of people's strivings is imbued by the propulsion of Cosmic Fire. Likewise, every thought generates tensions, and the creativeness of the spirit determines the shifting. Thus, when the essence of life strains the levers of shifting, all qualities disclose their correspondences. Therefore, when life is strained by multifold energies, the quality of energies must become receptive. The assertion of consciousness must intensify all qualities of energies. Thus is created a boundless quest.

448. When the history of a country is being laid, one has to construct as affirmatively as possible. As varying steps, historical constructions are being impregnated. Each historical step corresponds to the shifting of the Cosmic Magnet; thus, Our steps are so beautiful.

449. The spatial fires stratify all spheres. The rhythm of cosmic actions is unrestrainable. Man is affirmed as a recipient of spatial fires, but man denies all the higher laws. Therefore, when such lack of coordination becomes evident, the spatial fires cannot approach and begin their creative activity. Hence all the cosmic perturbations which are reacting on the planet. The influence of cosmic rays is twofold and is most powerful. The harmony of receptivity to the currents and the chaos in the assimilation create vital tides upon the planet.

450. Therefore, the spirit who assimilates all currents senses keenly the spatial fires. The chaos of the earthly sphere is so powerful that a purgatory has to be manifested. An Agni Yogi affirms these purifications. Hence, the Mother of Agni Yoga feels keenly all spatial purifications and the centers are therefore so tensed. Each energy unassimilated by humanity vibrates against the centers, and the sensitive heart absorbs everything.

451. The cosmic fires are imperceptible to the spirit who strives only toward the visible world. When the spirit is striving to the subtle spheres, the entire vastness of Cosmos unfolds before him. Therefore, the imperceptible cosmic fires are attracted to the creative spirit who perceives all the subtle energies. Thus, the principle of great creativity is built upon mutual attraction. The spatial fires are attracted into the orbit of cosmic strivings; hence, only the spirit who knows of the might of invisible forces can attract the cosmic fires. Thus is conformity effected. Thus is set up the cosmic creativity, with the highest coordination between the spirit and Cosmos.

452. All cosmic manifestations are permeated with mutual attraction. The Spatial Fire can be asserted only by the tension of the Magnet. Therefore, these currents can be affirmed only through cosmic attraction. A sensitive organism can reverberate to the tension of cosmic fires. Hence, each vibration in striving creates a channel for the Spatial Fire. If a link between the energies is affirmed, then a connection between the supermundane and earthly currents is established. Thus, the greatest coordination underlies the fiery assimilation of an Agni Yogi. Therefore, We strongly affirm the cosmic coordination. Thus everything enters into life.

453. When there is a real tendency toward the Cosmic Fire, a cosmic correlation is affirmed. Only when man will understand that the form of an action depends upon the impulse will the development of striving and the inner fire be affirmed, since it is impossible to establish correlation with the cosmic direction without an intensification of the higher principles. The entire lack of conformity results from these manifestations of imbalance. Each epoch is saturated by the cosmic fires and the qualities of human receptivity. Therefore, when the spirit does not ally himself with the cosmic fires a contrary current is set up. Thus, man determines his karma. This noncorrespondence is the sickness of the planet.

454. Only the causes of the cosmic fires can establish the balance. Thus, the knowledge of the currents affirmed by the Magnet directs one to true creativity.

The major part of human effort is set in the opposite direction. But each onrushing wave of a fiery spirit is heightened by correspondence. This is why the manifestations of the tension of the centers corresponds to the condition of spatial currents.

We, Brothers of Humanity, proclaim that the cosmic fires are subject to the receptivity of the fiery Agni Yogi. All currents pass through the centers. Therefore, all Our constructions are mighty ones. Thus, Our blended union is most powerful. Verily, We watch over the balance.

455. The cosmic correspondence strains all creative forces, and when the strings resound in conformity the cosmic tension can propound a creative formula. Thus, when the quality of the energy is consciously assimilated, constructiveness can be affirmed. Therefore, only the principle of correspondence can impart true striving. Only when the quality of the energy assimilates the properties of the cosmic fires is the higher correspondence affirmed. Thus, in each impulse one has to look for the quality of higher correspondence, and the entire power of action is held in the invisible world.

456. Correspondence tautens all centers of an Agni Yogi. This is why the organism so sensitively feels all cosmic currents and the condition of health has to be so carefully guarded. During the shiftings of cosmic currents, the centers feel every vibration; hence caution is needed.

457. Under the tension of cosmic power, most heterogeneous forces saturate the spheres. The creativity of Light thus puts under strain corresponding energies, but darkness creates its snares. Indeed, only the cosmic correspondence can create beauty. Hence, when the planet is completely saturated with the fire of shifting the quality of victorious energies can be asserted. Thus is the affirmation of cosmic energies being created.

458. Cosmic reconstruction requires combinations affirmed by correspondence. When a spirit responds to cosmic reconstructions, a link between Cosmos and man is being established. Hence, when the spirit creates together with Cosmos the cosmic link is affirmed. How can one be affirmed in the cosmic reconstruction? Only through the quality of correspondence. The quality of correspondence gives impetus to all cosmic constructions, and humanity proclaims in this way the testimony of the advance of its spirit. Thus, a limitless correspondence is being affirmed.

459. When a definite cosmic possibility is affirmed, all obstacles are intensified. Space then resounds with the tension of cosmic fires and the dark forces are very taut. Consequently, decisive battles take place. That is why We are not having so strenuous a period.

460. Cosmic reconstruction contains in itself all human strivings. When cosmic reconstruction saturates the planet, a cosmic stimulus strains the spirit. Thereupon, forces group themselves according to polarity and thus saturate the spheres around reconstruction. It is impossible to segregate human strivings from cosmic reconstruction. One and the same impulse motivates all the forces; hence, each sphere is steeped in the cosmic reconstruction. Thus, human reason can enter no complaint against Cosmos. In life, everything is built up from the principles of containment and correspondence, and the qualities of correspondence are boundless.

461. During the cosmic reconstruction there is apparent the manifestation of dark currents which oppose the Cosmic Magnet. Each wave of Light evokes

the tension of dark forces. Thus, the Cosmic Will is apparent in cosmic reconstruction. The gatekeepers of evil soak the cosmic reconstruction with asphyxiating gases, but in the cosmic reconstruction the power of Light becomes active transmuting Fire. Thus, Light burns the darkness. Thus, the cosmic reconstruction can be affirmed in Infinity.

462. The pull of the Cosmic Magnet induces magnetic storms in space. The earthly plane likewise calls forth the energies which liberate the spirit; and all earthly energies impart their potencies to space. Also, all the energies which have not yet been manifested saturate the space. This is why the spirit is so strained in search of the course of the Cosmic Magnet, and the orbit of action is thus mutually determined.

463. The unrest which strains the planetary forces affirms cosmic reconstruction and spiritual advancement. The moving of the spirit toward cosmic reconstruction is evoked by conscious striving. Thus, each force proceeding in step with the Cosmic Magnet must imbue the space with cosmic reconstruction. The Spatial fire intensifies all processes of life and all cosmic manifestations. Hence, the contact with the channel of the Cosmic Magnet impels the fiery spirit. The spheres of action are saturated by the energies of Infinity.

464. Contact with the current of the Cosmic Fire imparts a stimulus to the spirit; and a vital action is intensified by this vital Fire. Hence, the fiery Agni Yogi senses all cosmic perturbations and tautens all spatial threads. This is why the attraction to the Highest terrifies the enemies so greatly. Hence, when Our creative energies enter into life Our adversaries are strained in counteraction. Therefore, the Cosmic Right is being asserted.

465. The creativity of Cosmos brings the spatial

fires closer to the planet. Spiritual striving must tauten its threads and find the ways to the spatial fires. Hence, every constructive possibility is intensified by thought. The approach to the spiritual fires may be found when spiritual concordance is established. The imbalance on the planet is the result of the absence of this approach. Thus, the sickness of the planet is in its imbalance.

466. Vital action is intensified by the striving energy of the spirit. Only the affirmed magnet of the spirit can evoke the fire of creativeness to life, but humanity exerts its energies for the construction of steps which do not always proceed in line with the course of the Cosmic Magnet. Therefore, the affirmation of balance or imbalance depends upon the human spirit. Thus, each cosmic step is tensed by the spirit and is made with the lever of Fire. It is thus that a vital action enters into a cosmic orbit.

467. During cosmic reconstruction a vital action is intensified by the current of the Cosmic Magnet; hence, human efforts are greatly varied. When the tension of the Magnet induces concordance, the spirit is aware of its destinations, but when the cosmic orbit is not acknowledged by the spirit then certainly cosmic imbalance is intensified. Thus, each spirit makes its contribution, and the responsibility for the direction is in the spirit. That is why the dark forces and those of Light are under such strain and the battle is so great. Yes, yes, yes!

468. Upon the higher plane it is necessary to strive along with all the higher affirmations. Creativeness of the higher tension can affirm a cosmic power. The contacting of the spatial current is accessible to the spirit who is affirmed in cosmic affinity. Thus, only cosmic consciousness can give impetus to the human spirit.

469. Verily, all the tensions of the dark forces are

opposed to the Forces of Light. Therefore, the imbalance in Cosmos is definitely pronounced by the affirmation of battle. The adherence to the course of the Cosmic Magnet can saturate all strivings, but only the Forces of Light know the course leading to reconstruction. All opposing forces are therefore intensifying their currents.

470. Cosmic tension is reflected upon all planes, and transmutation of the spirit takes place on the planet. Only the power of thought can impart tension to the spirit, and transmutation of the spirit engulfs all that is weak. But the ascent is powerful for one who is in pace with the Cosmic Magnet. The cosmic creativity thus intensifies the striving quests. Therefore, the transmutation of the spirit strains all strata.

471. The affirmation of cosmic reconstruction intensifies all spatial fires. The acceptance of the basis of cosmic fires imparts a spiritual quality to the reconstruction. The creativeness of cosmic fires is intensified by the principle of magnetism. Hence, in the attraction of the Cosmic Magnet there is contained all cosmic creativeness. The creativity of Cosmos is linked with the tensity of cosmic fires, and the spiritual saturation of the planet depends upon the impulsion of the cosmic fires. Hence, humanity is under the strain of its own strivings; and the free will creates, affirming a cosmic urge or a contrary manifestation. Thus, when the spirit of humanity is attracted to the Cosmic Magnet the path of the spirit is found. The spirit thus strives into the Infinite.

472. Therefore, in the difficult days of cosmic reconstruction the dark ones are most tense; and when the Forces of Light assume power the Cosmos teems with opposing influences. Thus, Our Forces sat-

urate the space, but the dark ones endeavor to attain supremacy.

473. The cosmic reconstruction intensifies all spatial fires. Therefore, each will is subject to intense influences. Thus, when thought seeks a channel of action, its quality has the seed of an intense quest at its base. Hence, when thought is strained by the impellent force of the Magnet, the results can be assured. Thus, every energy that reaches the tensity emanating from the Magnet will be most powerful, for Light engulfs darkness. Thus, the building of evolution depends upon an inspiring trend of thought.

474. The quality of the energy imbues each action. According to the intensity of the action the tension of energy can be defined, but the quality of the energy lies in the seed of the spirit. The quality of action issues from the quality of striving. Hence, when the fiery impulse intensifies the creativeness of the spirit, the quality of the energy reaches a fiery height.

When nations set up their karmic courses, the quality of actions is saturated by a karmic striving of spirit. Thus, each spirit which creates its own karma draws from this treasury of spirit. Boundless and powerful is the creativeness of the spirit.

475. When the Cosmic Magnet strains all forces, the space begins to reverberate. Therefore, each force is heightened by the current of an intensified reverberation. In cosmic beginnings, it is important to know the affirmation of the Magnet and the quality of the energies in the spiritual strivings. All spiritual constructions sound a spatial keynote. Upon this keynote resound the subtle organisms. Thus does the creative keynote of the spirit act in space.

476. In the earthly spheres there are gases accumulated which help the discharge of cosmic whirlwinds

and also the spiritual shiftings. The earthly spheres are greatly encumbered with various exertions. Space is the arena of the Great Battle! Verily, there is no spot which is not alive with fiery sparks!

477. Each wave of Common Good is intensified by the Forces of Light, and also by counteractions. The manifestations of light and shade pertains to the whole of Cosmos. Hence, each wave of Common Good induces a saturation with various currents. Each propelled wave intensifies the creative impulses, and the human task is to find the direction of the Cosmic Magnet by propelling the thoughts toward the Common Good. Thus, thought creates in space. Limitless are the ways of evolution.

478. The cosmic orbit comprises the attractions of all creative energies. Each quality of energy has its impulsion, and life is intensified through these energies. The explosions which fill the space occur from noncoordination. Hence, each conscious energy produces coordination. When the Cosmic Magnet calls to action, the attraction spreads through space and imbues all impulses of propelled energies. Thus does life propel its basic attractions.

479. There cannot be the manifestation of life in Cosmos without the vital forces provided by the Origins. Verily, the power of the Origins spiritualizes the forces. Therefore, the power of the Mother of the World imbues all Space.

480. The creativeness of the Cosmic Magnet aggregates all the best energies. The quality of the energy attracts to its seed corresponding energies. Hence, the saturation of space depends so greatly upon the quality of striving. To such an extent does the quality of each impulse establish the manifestation of action that its basic quality is its very impulse. Thus, the thought of humanity is determined by the striving that is in the impulse. The only way to realization of the creativeness of the Cosmic Magnet is the cognizance of most subtle Fire at its base. Thus is Infinity affirmed.

481. At the foundation of Our works lies subtle Fire. Thus, Our creative striving is in pace with the Cosmic Magnet. All Our undertakings proceed with the Cosmic Magnet.

482. Only in the name of Truth should the very combative impulses be heightened. Only in the name of Truth can the most saturated fires be heightened. Certainly, each energy issuing from the cognizance of the Great Cosmic Plan attracts cosmic fires. Each conscious thought is attracted into the orbit of the Cosmic Plan. Therefore, every effort in the name of Truth will be crowned with victory. Thus is Infinity built.

483. During the building of cosmic structures all outer decisions are tensed by inner fires. During the shiftings all forces which must depart are strained by the quality inherent in the designated fire. Therefore, the forces which come into life must saturate each manifested opposition with their fires. Thus, the entire cosmic construction is based upon transmutation, and the creativeness of Cosmos is perpetually transmuting.

484. Nothing can withstand the transmuting Fire, but the enemies cling to the last pillars. Therefore, Our transmuting Power ascends with the Cosmic Magnet, and all Our exertions will conquer through the saturation of Space. Thus do We create.

485. Each possibility that is set aside is subject to cosmic tension. The Cosmic Will saturates all tensed possibilities, and each wave attracts multiple propelled energies. Therefore, the contact of the Magnet with the cosmic orbit attracts new energies from the Space. Thus does the cosmic transmutation intensify all creative forces. Only by this great law can evolution be impelled forward. Thus is the vast cosmic evolution constructed.

486. The expansion of consciousness comprises all conceptions which lead to evolution. Faith in the transmutation of all energies provides the understanding of all new movements. When the spirit is imbued with the significance of cosmic transmutation it can be conceived to what an extent cosmic evolution depends upon the shifting of the degrees of consciousness. The significance of all shiftings must enter into the consciousness. The tension of the striving spirit results in an intense quest for new paths. Thus are the steps of evolution built.

487. When the spirit is able to dwell in the spheres void of earthly pressure, he can indeed reveal all acquisitions. Earthly conditions are so encumbered that it is impossible to reveal all qualities of the inner energies. When manifesting an urge to an earthly battle, the subtle centers must be protected. Therefore, such tension must be lived through in all caution.

488. When striving for personal ends exceeds the affirmation of striving for humanity, then nothing can shift the consciousness. Therefore, each manifested evidence of personal striving tenses a lever which affirms only the reverse of cosmic tension. Consequently, when the enemies imbue the space with their cravings the Cosmic Magnet strains its levers. Thus is Infinity built.

489. The orbit of the Cosmic Magnet comprises the entire cosmic evolution. The creativity of the Cosmic Magnet depends on those tensions which are imbued by Fire. Thus a fiery saturation is implicit in each action, and in the coordination of the fires and the striving the entire creative process is laid. Hence,

the spirit must strive to the cognizance of his fires, and if he finds a conformity between the cosmic course and his own striving he may become a co-worker of the Cosmic Magnet. Vigilantly must the spirit follow the magnetic course and direct his own fires. Thus, the spirit must strive consciously to create his own fiery orbit.

490. Beautiful is the orbit of the spirit which knows its own destination. The direction of each spirit must be goal-fitting, but each spirit must know the affirmed law of evolution.

491. The regeneration of the spirit is achieved through striving, not through the monotony in skills which beclouds one's mind. Evenness is usualness; evenness is numbness; evenness is death of spirit. Only when the spirit understands its line of action can it set itself into the orbit of the cosmic course.

Why, then, is the spirit tempered through various exertions? The beauty of the tempering of spirit is contained in the potential of striving. Therefore, when the spirit strives in quest of the Source the evenness of life is interrupted. In eliminating evenness one can attain the unusual. In this, humanity must affirm itself. The entire beauty and creativity of the Lords is built upon the unusual. The aspiration of humanity toward the unusual will give it the understanding of the New, and will advance it toward Infinity.

492. The attainment of the Common Good is affirmed through the search for the course of the Cosmic Magnet. Only when the spirit can contact the cosmic current, can it reach the understanding of the higher law. The course of the Cosmic Magnet carries the Fire of Space, which effects the reverberation of the Cosmic Magnet. Hence, each possibility in step with the Cosmic Magnet reaches toward the Common

Good. This conformity is held to be the possibility for a striving quest. Hence, the key to the Common Good is contained in the quest of the spirit. Thus, each powerful tension provides a key to the Common Good.

493. When the spirit adheres to the Common Good, all paths are open to it and each wave of displacement is accepted as an offering. When the spirit strives to cooperate with the Cosmic Magnet, the expanded consciousness can provide a circle of action. Hence, besides the spatial impulse one must cognize one's own striving. Thus is Infinity built.

494. All laws which lead to confirmation of the shifting are based upon the Common Good. Each new energy is projected into space for the acquiring of a creative quality. Energies are thus propelled from chaos, and each cosmic current can bestow creativeness. The shifting is confirmed only by the principle of the Cosmic Magnet. There where the power of the Cosmic Magnet functions, goal-fitness is at work. Hence, it may be affirmed that when the old is being replaced by the new the cosmic goal-fitness applies vital laws.

495. When the tension of the Carriers of Fires is revealed as a shifting power, the tension of the opposing forces increases. Therefore, all the measures taken by the enemies are in proportion to the growth of tension. Every wall erected by the enemy must crumble under the cyclone of his own errors. Thus, the enemies are saturated with their own poisons. Our Carriers of Fires are tensed cosmically, and victory is inevitable. Thus, the world will know all the obstacles encountered by the Carriers of Fires. The fire of spirit imbues the space.

496. The Higher Force is always tensed in creation in conformity with the universal energies. When the shifting requires the highest tension, the Guardians of Higher Tasks fulfill the higher mission. The creativeness of Light sets up corresponding affirmations. The constructiveness of the Guardians of Light seeks goal-fitness. Thus, the constructivity of the Higher Forces proceeds in highest concordance, and Infinity cosmically guards all tasks.

497. What monstrous thoughts are speeding through space! What engenderments are obscuring the Voice of Light! Humanity does not ponder upon the thought forms which man himself has to redeem. Space is impregnated by men's thoughts, and everything is being correspondingly attracted. Consequently, the engenderments of thought spin the Karma of humanity, and the quality of action is in conformity with the striving. Thus, humanity must strive limitlessly to redeem itself.

498. As a counterbalance to these engenderments, the fiery spirits build the structures of Light. Hence, as the opposition to darkness, the Carriers of Fires create the best karmic actions. This is why Our Carriers of Fires are so strained. Our Mother of Agni Yoga vibrates in all centers. Thus, We create a new step. Thus, We enhance the best possibilities.

499. The energy of the engenderments establishes each consequence in turn. Each monstrous thought brings to man pregnant defeat. Each thought attracting the manifestation of defeat can create an atmosphere of cosmic perturbations. Hence, one must strive consciously and prudently to creativeness. Thus, conscious striving will bring the cognition of Infinity.

500. A sensitive Agni Yogi knows all paths to the realization of Infinity. The spirit-knowledge reads the Book of Life, and the wisdom of ages is deposited as accumulations in the Chalice. Therefore, the law of unification is contained in the synthesis of the Chalice. Upon this knowledge We build Our wondrous step. We have molded Our life over millennia. The cosmic laws are beautiful. Thus, into the seed of the spirit is laid the beauty of Be-ness.

501. The law of sacrifice demands of humanity the offering of its best elements. When the spirit of man will grasp the fact that striving for the higher achievement is the most essential action, he will cling to the Cosmic Magnet; and the concept of sacrifice will then take on the meaning of service to the Highest Reason. Cosmic creativeness applies the most powerful levers for evolution, and the spirit senses the application of the best energies. When the affirmation of life consciousness awakens all subtle faculties the law of sacrifice is then understood as the highest achievement.

502. Those in Our Service who have realized the power of sacrifice know the beauty of achievement. Therefore, they will achieve who have realized the Service in their hearts. Thus, Service, in the name of a powerful achievement, bestows beauty upon existence. All karmic effects are forged from the blendings of spirit strivings, and all strivings are inscribed in the Book of Life. Thus, lives are being built and the beauty of Be-ness is defined.

503. In the Book of Life one must look for the manifestations leading to the concept of the Higher Existence. Therefore, only the application of correlation leads to the goal-fitness of actions. Why, then, does humanity struggle so greatly in the constant effort to redeem the effects of its own engenderments? Each concordance brings its affirmation. Thus, each possibility saturated with striving leads to harmony and intensifies the fires of the spirit. In this tense battle the channels of spirit and heart are affirmed. Therefore, in Our creativity We strain these channels. Thus We create the better possibilities.

504. In the Book of Life is inscribed each energy which is moved by the impulse of the spirit. The quality of the energy is predetermined by a karmic effect. Space is filled with these karmic effects and each atmospheric stream is intensified by these energies. Therefore, the redemption of its deeds by humanity demands purification. The Book of Life contains all cosmic preordinations. Creativity is correlated with striving, and striving leads toward the cosmic course if the torches of quest are kindled. Hence, each page leading to the realization of the Cosmic Magnet is a better page, and the searching spirit will open the gates to the foundations of Be-ness. Thus is Infinity built.

505. When a spirit strives to inscribe a better page in the Book of Life his acceptance of the service for the Common Good opens to him all gates. Hence, when the thought of the flaming Agni Yogi imbues the space, then verily the spirit creates with Cosmos. Thus is the higher concordance established. Therefore, in this battle Our enemies fear greatly the higher concordance, but Our victory will be the more powerful.

506. In the proclaimed law of life the principle of harmony is truly majestic! Often the spirit ascribes his action to a good motive whereas the power of the spirit is impelled in the opposite direction. Thus think those who do not wish to look straight ahead toward the Light. By such thinking the spirit admits lack of will, and lack of will is chaos. Since we know that effects proceed from causes, each spirit must examine his own motives. The entire Book of Life is concerned with the qualities of motives.

507. In the Book of Life is contained the saturated stream of creative fire. Only upon the higher law can the page of Sublime Be-ness be affirmed. Valiantly must the spirit strive to the realization of all the subtle principles in order to attain higher knowledge. The Book of Life contains every aspiring action. The Book of Life contains the manifestation of all vital fires. The heart carries in itself all imprints of the Book of Life. The heart carries in itself the beauty of Be-ness and boundless cognition. Verily, the attainment of the heart affirms all possibilities. Verily, the attainment of the heart forges all the best steps.

508. When by the power of Light the property of darkness is surpassed, the affirmation of the ray of Truth enters life. When the ray issues from the potential the striving spirit attracts all fires. Therefore, when humanity will understand the power in the quality of thought it will master the mightiest lever. Humanity must strive indefatigably to the realization of this mighty lever.

509. The entire evolution proceeds in cosmic tension. The power of the spirit creates in cosmic tension. The great Universal Mystery is fulfilled in cosmic tension. The cosmic action can be created only in the attraction of correspondences. Thus, concordance intensifies all cosmic actions, and the maximum of tension gives the maximum of action.

510. The creation of the great shifting requires the affirmation of the best tensions. The great affirmation imbues the entire space, and it is contained in the principle of attraction. All the laws are confirmed through fiery attraction, and all cosmic principles are imbued with the unity of Fire. Full coordination effects full harmony, and the attraction between particles belonging to one seed is powerfully imbued by the law of blending. Thus, the fiery Cosmic Will saturates all lives. All vital principles of creativeness are governed

by the law of blending. Thus, We create and reveal the foundations of Be-ness.

511. How can a law be immutable? How does a law create? How does a law cumulate? By its powerful consonance. If consciousness leads to the affirmation of Cosmic Right, likewise cosmic power attracts toward the seed. Hence, life is affirmed by the Cosmic Reason in Cosmic Right. When all centers reverberate, there is affirmed that harmony which is more powerful than any creative energy. Thus, the highest potentiality saturates the power of cosmic blending.

Verily, Agni Yoga is given to humanity, but the centers of concordance are given for the higher blendings.

512. Creation through the integrated heart attracts all power. Creation through the integrated spirit attracts all the best energies. Even countless inventions are concerned with the power of unification. Why, then, not accept that the creativity of the Great Plan is saturated with the impulse of unification. Thus, all the mighty energies are created through the attraction of concordance with the Cosmic Magnet. The striving spirit finds its way to concordance. Thus is the saturation of space in operation.

513. The lofty Agni Yoga is given for the affirmation of the great concordance. Vital action is imbued with all fires. Thus is each energy introduced into life, and thus is great Matter united with the spiritual centers. Thus, concordance is enforced by the ray.

514. Life attains consummation in creativity, and the Book of Life is filled with heterogeneous energies. In fiery striving the spirit finds response. In fiery striving the heart receives a responding vibration. In the beauty of the spirit there lies the realization of the entire might of cosmic consummation. Thus, the joy of Be-ness attracts the spirit to consummation. It is

inscribed in the Book of Life that the direct path to consummation leads through the heart. Thus, the cosmic law intensifies the spiritual impulses, and the life of space resounds in beauty.

The Book of Life tells of the majesty of the law of unification and of all the sublime energies that are blended in this law. Out of the great impulses the spirit intensifies mightily the impulse of self-sacrifice, and in this fire do we achieve consummation. The more mightily, the more fiery!

515. The Cosmic Magnet is intensified by the impellent Fire. The extent to which humanity through the expansion of consciousness can accept the direction of the Magnet depends upon the striving of the spirit. Only this lever can indicate the way to the magnet of Fire. Only the quest of the spirit can give a direction to the Source of energy. Thus can one affirm coordination and propel the spirit toward Truth.

516. The quality of energies strains the creative impulses. The freely manifested will is strained by the quality of energies. Each creative thought is attracted to the fiery focus. Each creative tension attracts the corresponding fiery energies. Therefore, all actions must have striving at their foundation, and the higher quality of energies is revealed in the creativeness of the spirit.

517. The affirmation of the law of correspondence depends upon the tension of the forces of spirit. How can one be affirmed in the understanding of the law of correspondence if the spirit does not accept the impulse of Fire! Only in a limitless seeking does the spirit intensify his strivings, fierily saturated.

518. The orbit of human actions strives to conformity with the cosmic course. Each spark of the spirit can be kindled by adherence to the Fire of Space.

Why do men thus lock themselves within their own orbits? In the orbit of actions are contained all the impulses needed to reach the Cosmic Magnet. The creativeness of the Cosmic Magnet impels humanity toward Truth, and the sensitiveness of the spirit gives knowledge of the direction.

I am trying to bring you closer to Infinity, not merely to give you an exquisite concept but so that you may acquire refinement of consciousness. If through the knowledge of causes we expand our consciousness, then through the cognition of quality we refine it. This property, and the quality of thought and feeling, will evince the cognition of the origins of creation.

Words cannot formulate what constitutes high quality of thinking. But each one, even he who labors, senses its required quality. This quality, as a aeolian harp, resounds to the current of reality; and it accumulates beneath the center of the Chalice the subtlest soma of cognition and discernment, not only by means of co-measurement but also in accordance with immutability.

This last spark of Truth kindles the attracting Beacon of Light.

At so dark a moment, let us dwell upon the Light!

AGNI YOGA SERIES

Leaves of Morya's Garden I (The Call)	1924
Leaves of Morya's Garden II (Illumination)	1925
New Era Community	1926

Signs of Agni Yoga

Agni Yoga	1929
Infinity I	1930
Infinity II	1930
Hierarchy	1931
Heart	1932
Fiery World I	1933
Fiery World II	1934
Fiery World III	1935
Aum	1936
Brotherhood	1937
Supermundane (in 3 volumes)	1938

Agni Yoga Society
www.agniyoga.org

www.ingramcontent.com/pod-product-compliance
Lightning Source LLC
Chambersburg PA
CBHW061651040426
42446CB00010B/1691